The INNOVATOR
Next Door

50 Stories of Creative Inspiration to Spark New In-the-Box Thinking

JOHN MCCARTHY, PH.D.

Copyright © 2020 by John McCarthy Ph.D.

All rights reserved.

No part of this book may be reproduced, Scanned, or distributed in any printed or electronic form without express written permission from the author.

ISBN 978-1-939237-75-0

Published by Suncoast Digital Press, Inc.
Sarasota, Florida, U.S.A.

*Dedicated to my brother Pat (1948–2017),
an extraordinarily special creative role model in life
who taught, inspired, and nurtured me in
optimism, resilience, and laughter.*

Contents

Preface ix
Introduction xiii
1   Let's Look at Creativity Questions 1
2   CQ: What Can Fill a Hole? 3
3   CQ: How Can Passengers Move Through Airports More Efficiently? 5
4   CQ: How Can I Help Others See a New Perspective? 7
5   CQ: Can Urine Help People Who Are Refugees? 9
6   CQ: What Happens to Those Crayons that Came with Dinner? 11
7   CQ: How Could a Suicide Attempt Be Prevented? 13
8   CQ: How Can Tourists Be Attracted to a Place 200 Kilometers North of the Arctic Circle? 15
9   CQ: How Might I Find a Product to Sell that I Believe In? . . .17
10 CQ: How Can More People Become Interested in Sweden? . .19
11 CQ: How Does a Pinecone Relate to Reading? 21
12 CQ: Does Driving in the Rain Have to Be So Risky? 23
13 CQ: How Might the Frequency of Alcohol Addiction Be Decreased? 25
14 CQ: How Can Airlines Get Passengers' Attention in Flight? . .27
15 CQ: How Might Entrepreneurial Skills Be Taught? 29
16 CQ: How Might People Living in Poverty Be Helped? 31
17 CQ: How Can My Time Be of Value to Others? 33
18 CQ: Paper or Plastic or…? 35
19 CQ: How Else Can Barbers Uplift a Community? 37
20 CQ: How Can More Customers Be Drawn to a Restaurant? . .39
21 CQ: How Can I Send a Letter Without Knowing the Address? 41

22 CQ: Where Can I Look for New Ideas?. 43
23 CQ: How Might the Olympics Inspire Other Populations?. . .45
24 CQ: Is There a Word for That? 47
25 CQ: How Can Food Mix with Social Change? 49
26 CQ: Can a Hotel Be Put on Wheels? 51
27 CQ: What Else Can a Library Offer? 53
28 CQ: Can Rivers, Lakes, and Oceans Be Made Cleaner? 55
29 CQ: Are There Other Ways to Land Airplanes?. 57
30 CQ: How Can Older Adults Be More Active? 59
31 CQ: Are Coffee Grounds Really Just Waste? 61
32 CQ: Is Vision Necessary to Play Baseball?. 63
33 CQ: How Can I Find My Car in a City of
   Three Million People?. 65
34 CQ: How Can a Better Vacuum Cleaner Be Made?. 67
35 CQ: How Can I, an Experienced Golfer,
   Keep Improving My Golf Skills? 69
36 CQ: How Can an Expected Outcome Be
   Changed for the Better? 71
37 CQ: How Can I See The World in a Different Way? 73
38 CQ: What Could Prevent a Person from Stealing a Bicycle?. .75
39 CQ: How Can Prison Time Be More Worthwhile? 77
40 CQ: How Can We Detect the Cause of an Airplane Crash?. . .79
41 CQ: How Can People Be Encouraged to Buy a Used Car?. . .81
42 CQ: If We Can Locate Satellites from Earth,
   Can We Locate Earth Objects from Space?. 83
43 CQ: How Do I Find the Person of My Dreams? 85
44 CQ: What Can I Learn from the Efficiency of a Pit Crew?. . .87
45 CQ: How Can an Elderly Person Find a
   Home Away from Home? 89

46 CQ: How Can Depression Be Addressed
   in a Community with Limited Resources? 91
47 CQ: How Can Time Be Reversed? 95
48 CQ: How Does Chess Interact with Opportunity in Youth?. . .97
49 CQ: How Can Observation Help Me to Assist Others? 99
50 CQ: How Might a Compliment Alter a Stressful Situation? . 101
51 CQ: How Can Art Help Solve Community Problems? 103
52 Becoming the Innovator Next Door. 105
Acknowledgments 109
About the Author. 111

Preface

I sometimes begin my creativity workshops with a few examples like these:

- I once read that, long ago, people in China would place firecrackers on their kitchen floors. Why would they do such a thing? (Answer: The firecrackers served as a fire alarm system. Quite creative, eh?)
- On March 12, 1990, something spectacular took place. There was a head-on collision between two Chrysler LeBarons on Route 640 in Virginia. Both cars were damaged, yet both drivers sustained only minor injuries. What is so special about that? (Answer: It was the first known accident involving two cars in which both had driver's side airbags.)
- At the end of a meal, an airline passenger was seen putting salt and pepper on the chocolate cake. "Oh, no," the flight attendant said to the passenger. "You know that you don't need to do that, right?" "Oh, in fact, this cake needs salt and pepper," the passenger replied, "if I'm going to avoid eating it." (Certainly a creative way to avoid desserts.)
- I once read about a third-grade class reviewing material from their science class. "Who knows the parts of the atom?" the teacher asked. One student raised their hand and enthusiastically said, "Protons, neutrons, and croutons." (A fine example of unintended creativity!)

This book is the culmination of my passions in life: creative thinking and problem-solving, current events, and people's paths in life. In writing it, I initially debated the best audience for it. Who would be interested? *Who is helped by inspiring stories of creative thinking?* My answer—and maybe "bias" is a better word here—is most everyone. I am a strong believer that the world needs more creative thinkers and problem-solvers, particularly with the life issues and global challenges in our future.

Yet, an audience of "everyone" isn't the whole answer. This book is for people who relish stories and have an *itch*. It was written for people living in story-driven careers: educators, clergy members, advertisers, marketers, screenwriters, entrepreneurs, coaches, media professionals, and mental health professionals. They tell stories, share stories, and create stories. They have that itch to find ideas for a whole host of reasons. Perhaps it's to help clients. Maybe it's a matter of improving their brand. Possibly it's to grab a student's or reader's attention. Anyone whose intention is to persuade others knows that stories are their best tools.

And the itch could be in your personal life. Something that is bugging you—that small problem that needs some kind of fix. A better way to wash those dishes. A way to keep the squirrels from invading the bird feeder. The way your packages are delivered. The way your toothbrush is designed. Linkner (2011) related a story told by a nonprofit director of an entrepreneurial academy who encouraged people to look for "dangnabbits," those frustrating moments that arise around a situation or product. Keep a list of those "dangnabbits," Linkner encouraged, as they can be a reservoir of creative flashes.

In a recent survey of nearly 50,000 people, it became clear that creativity is used in helpful ways. Over half of participants said that it helped them think about problems and emotions. Over two-thirds of individuals indicated that it aided them in their self-esteem, and over three-quarters of respondents related that creative activities were a tool to put stress on the back burner (BBC News, 2019). More broadly, creativity has global benefits. According to the World Economic Forum, the demand for creative goods such as film and fashion more than doubled between 2002 and 2015 (Whiting, 2019). Yet, being creative in our thinking and problem-solving is not easy. Adopting a creative mindset takes discipline and persistence in maintaining our curiosity about the world. On the one hand, 85% of American adults believe that creative thinking skills are critical to their jobs, yet 32% are uncomfortable in applying creative thinking in their workplaces (Jana, 2012). At the same time, relatively few people in the United States have had formal coursework or training in creative skills. In fact, 71% of respondents in the same survey indicated that creativity should be offered as a course.

Yet good news is evident. A Gallup study of K–12 teachers found a link between creativity in the classroom and students who were more confident and engaged (2019). Teachers integrating creativity into assignments were more likely than their colleagues to indicate that their students took more responsibility in learning and were more open to taking risks (Saad, 2019). The vast majority of teachers (87%) and parents (77%) expressed a belief that incorporating creativity into assignments will offer rewards for students (Gallup, 2019).

The United Nations marks its World Creativity and Innovation Day every April 21 (United Nations, n.d.). The people in this book didn't wait until that date to foster positive change in their neighborhoods, their communities, or the world. They simply started, and it is my hope that these 50 stories fuel your hope, your inspiration, and your creative thinking as you perhaps seek to do the same.

Sources

BBC News. (2019, May 8). *Getting creative really does boost your mood, survey suggests*. https://www.bbc.com/news/entertainment-arts-48188508

Gallup, Inc. (2019). *Creativity in learning*. https://www.gallup.com/education/267449/creativity-learning-transformative-technology-gallup-report-2019.aspx

Jana, R. (2012, November 15). *Adobe survey: Creativity is important for career success*. https://www.zdnet.com/article/adobe-survey-creativity-is-important-for-career-success/

Linkner, J. (2011). *Disciplined dreaming: A proven system to drive breakthrough creativity*. Jossey-Bass.

Saad, L. (2019, October 28). *Teachers who promote creativity see educational results*. Gallup. https://news.gallup.com/opinion/gallup/245600/teachers-promote-creativity-educational-results.aspx

United Nations. (n.d.). *World Creativity and Innovation Day 21 April*. https://www.un.org/en/observances/creativity-and-innovation-day

Whiting, K. (2019, April 18). *5 things you need to know about creativity*. World Economic Forum. https://www.weforum.org/agenda/2019/04/5-things-you-need-to-know-about-creativity/

Introduction

Two people are riding an escalator when it suddenly stops. Exasperated, they start yelling out for help: "There are two people STUCK on an escalator, and we NEED HELP. Now, would SOMEBODY PLEASE DO SOMETHING?" But the building is empty.

After a seemingly long wait, they hear someone coming—a maintenance worker is coming up from a floor below! "Hello? Hey, don't worry about it—I'll fix it in a second." He's riding his escalator up, and it, too, suddenly comes to an inexplicable halt. Now all three are stuck with no hope of rescue—unless they change their way of thinking.[1]

Have you ever seen anyone with such stuck thinking? It's silly to imagine being stuck on an escalator when it can easily double as stairs. But perhaps thinking is stuck in other ways that are harder to recognize, let alone resolve. Finding a way off individual escalators is a task that can be assisted by others' experiences and stories.

Stories surround us daily. We check our phone and end up with stories on Facebook, a newspaper app, or a YouTube video. We walk into a library, and stories abound in newspapers, magazines, and books. A visit to the theater for a movie reveals another plot. The local high school is putting on a musical where a story comes out in song. Stories make us cry, laugh, think, and learn. They help to release emotion, make meaning of the world, and assist people with transitions in life (Gladding & Wallace, 2010). Stories cross borders, and, as Gladding and Wallace noted, "Storytelling is one of the few human traits common to all cultures" (2010, p. 15). People would rather hear a story than a statistic (Kida, 2006).

---

[1] This is a summary of a Canadian television commercial. "Stuck on an elevator—Take action." Retrieved from https://www.youtube.com/watch?v=47rQkTPWW2I.

People have become "storytelling creatures" (Kida, 2006, p. 16) in many facets of life. Some people are in storytelling professions without even realizing it—educators, academics, counselors, consultants, trainers, comedians, and journalists. All spend considerable time composing and listening to stories. Visits with friends entail stories. Relaying symptoms to your physician is a kind of life story, and a meeting with a lawyer about being wronged embeds a story (Seelig, 2015). Stories in fact are a part of successful ideas, according to Heath and Heath (2007), and listening to others' stories can serve as a learning experience, "a kind of mental flight simulator," that helps in a faster, more effective response to situations (p. 18).

This book celebrates stories—stories of people who creatively think and problem-solve, people who don't let themselves get stuck on an escalator. Creative problem-solving has been a passion of mine since I was a child. I was fascinated with how people around me—siblings, friends, teachers, and coaches—came up with ideas, seemingly out of thin air. One of my older brothers, and the person to whom I've dedicated this book, was particularly rich in resourcefulness. When we were kids, he would spontaneously come up with fun little games, practical jokes, quick challenges ("I bet you can't stand on one foot and balance a book on your head"), and insightful ways to solve problems. This book is meant to add to your story repertoire, whether personal or professional, and hopefully add ideas, options, and inspiration to your life.

Creative Problem-Solving (CPS): When Familiar Doesn't Work

Have you ever seen a *Toy Story* or *Star Wars* movie? If so, the automatic question is, "Well, of course, but which one do you mean?" Sequels to movies such as *Toy Story* or *Star Wars* are made because people will buy tickets. They know the story, the plot, and the characters. It's familiar. If I see one, I may be more inclined to go to the next. And the next. And the…well, you get the idea. We like the familiar because it's easier—there's less of a burden on us to learn a new situation.

Our brains also like the familiar. We spend a good amount of our brain money buying—or thinking about—the same things over and over. You may find yourself thinking about how English class stinks, how the Red Sox can win the next World Series, or how that person in middle school broke your heart years ago.

When it comes to problems, our brains also often turn to the familiar, particularly to what worked before. It makes sense, right? If these actions helped before in solving this problem, then they would work again. It is perfectly plausible.

But not always…

What happens when those past problem-solving successes *don't* work? In such moments, we can turn to creativity, specifically **creative problem-solving (CPS)**. CPS has been defined as "a process, a method, a system for approaching a problem in an imaginative way resulting in effective action" (Noller, 1979, pp. 4–5). In other words, CPS can be used to approach and address a new type of challenge—one that is unfamiliar.

CPS skills, then, are critical to successfully navigating new situations, yet obtaining these skills may take some real effort. In attempting to solve challenges in life, it is easy to rely—maybe even *over-rely*—on those tools that brought success to past problems. Encountering a new problem with old tools may end up being akin to frustratingly trying to get that square peg into a round hole. As hard as the effort to succeed might be, it simply won't work. This type of effort brings to mind that famous line about insanity being a repetition of the same thing and expecting different results. According to Harvard Medical School research, about 60–80% of adults find the process of thinking "differently" to be uncomfortable (as cited by Dyer & Gregersen, 2011).

Many people associate creative thinking with thinking "out of the box." This phrase originated with a study of the nine-dot problem: imagine a square image of nine dots on a page in a tic-tac-toe format. The goal in this problem is to connect all nine dots in four consecutive lines without lifting your pen from the paper. Give yourself a moment and try it. You will likely find it challenging, though "frustrating" and "maddening" may also describe the experience. This test has been around a while—decades, actually—and can still make the most patient people perturbed.

If you weren't successful with connecting the nine dots, please don't be concerned. In fact, you are in the vast majority, as research has found that very few people get it correct without some assistance, though it is possible to solve. One solution to the nine-dot problem—spoiler alert—is to extend a line *outside of the box*, that is, beyond the confines of the dots. Thus, the phrase "out-of-the-box thinking" was born.

Thinking at the Edges of the Box

Though out-of-the-box thinking may be very commonly associated with creativity, I maintain that getting out of the box is *not* necessary for creative problem-solving. Yes, go outside of the dots and outside of the box for the transformative creativity of an Einstein, but don't be discouraged if you're not in his category. (In fact, welcome to the club!)

In everyday life, let's put those dots aside and look at the box in a new way. If the box represents our foreseeable range of options in a given situation, it's not practical to expect people to always be thinking outside of the box. Instead, we need to explore our options and push ourselves to the edges of the box, where creative ideas and options can be discovered. **Thinking on the fringes of the box is critically important to everyday creativity.**

A metaphor may help here. Football, soccer, hockey, basketball, badminton, tennis, volleyball, and ping pong—what do all of these have in common?

When the ball, puck, or shuttlecock goes out of bounds, you hear a referee whistle. You may hear a reaction from the crowd. You may see the players respond accordingly. Perhaps the clock stops. And one thing is inevitable: *play comes to halt*. In sports, the action happens within boundaries, within a box—often literally a box painted on a field or court. If you take that boundary away, it's a totally different game.

Oftentimes, the most strategic, most successful moves happen on the edges of the court—the boundary between playing and not playing at all. Wide receivers in football practice catching passes with both feet in bounds. Tennis pros try to land their shots on the line. Baseball is called "the game of inches" with its first- and third-base lines. The edge of the box is the place newbies fear because they don't want to step out of line and lose a point. Yet it's the place that, when learned to utilize well, offers great rewards.

When it comes to creative thinking, approach the sidelines, get close to the foul line, aim for the edge, and creative options will flow. Stay in bounds, and you'll find that creative thinking can sizzle.

Take Juan Metzger, for instance. The headline of his *New York Times* obituary in 1998 didn't mention his military service as an interrogator of prisoners of war for the Army in World War II. It didn't highlight his award as "Marketer of the Decade" in the 1970s, and it didn't point out his "unsuccess" in 1942 with a $2,000 campaign aimed at yogurt as a substitute for meat. No, the obituary read, "Juan Metzger, 79, is Dead: He Put the Fruit in Yogurt" (King, 1998). Mr. Metzger gets the credit for putting fruit at the bottom of the yogurt cup—strawberry being the first—and making yogurt a regular staple of the American (and perhaps your specific) diet. His creativity ran the sidelines in a simple, yet wonderful way. Yogurt and fruit were within Metzger's realm, and, when exploring the edge of the box, he found a new way to combine them and get them to customers.

When on the periphery, you can see things that no one may have noticed before. Madson (2005) explained, "It is a widespread belief that 'thinking out of the box'…means going after far-out and unusual ideas. A true understanding of this phrase means seeing what is really obvious, but until then, unseen.…Try thinking inside the box. Look more carefully" (pp. 62–63). That's what people featured in the following stories were able to do. They didn't transform the world in a way that, say, Edison did, but their edge-of-the-box thinking addressed a problem-opportunity with thought-provoking solutions that, at least to some extent, worked. In some cases, their creativity may in fact touch your life today.

The Innovator Next Door

This book is a collection of stories and situations where questions, problems, or problem-opportunities led to an idea on the edge of the box. You won't be reading about the brilliance of Marie Curie, George Washington Carver, or Johann Sebastian Bach. Instead, you will be gaining insights related to what French writer Georges Perec called the "infra-ordinary," the converse of the extraordinary events at the top of our individual newsfeeds (Walker, 2019). The infra-ordinary, or everyday innovators, are people who have had an impact, but who are not necessarily widely known. For people like you and me, their level of influence is more within reach than, say, the influence of Steve Jobs. We can call them the "innovator next door."

Another way to look at it is through the work of Beghetto and Kaufman (Kaufman & Beghetto, 2009; Beghetto & Kaufman, 2013), who proposed four levels of creativity in their model: mini-c, little-c, Pro-C, and Big-C.

Mini-c can be typified by your singing in the shower; little-c is a YouTube video of your singing; Pro-C is your songs hitting iTunes and being downloaded internationally; and Big-C is visiting Cleveland, Ohio, for your induction into the Rock and Roll Hall of Fame (Kaufman, 2016). The innovators on the following pages typically fall in the middle of the spectrum. The effects of their creativity reach well beyond mini-c, yet, for the most part, they aren't household names (Big-C).

The examples of innovation in this book are rich examples of "everyday creativity," which hovers around the little-c realm in Beghetto and Kaufman's model. An idea that dates to the 1980s, everyday creativity was initially proposed by Richards, Kinney, and others at the Harvard Medical School (Flora, 2009). More recently, Richards defined it as "our originality of everyday life" (Kaufman, 2019, 4:19)—something basic to survival. Everyday creativity includes getting sufficient food to eat, finding a child who was lost, and navigating life after a new move. It is more of the "how," rather than the "what," and it features flexibility, improvisation, and experience with different choices (Richards, 2007). Linkner (2011) described everyday creativity as "small changes in high frequency that add up to big results" that alter the way a person or a company think in their daily routines (p. 27). In business settings, examples include improving customer relation calls or making staff meetings more worthwhile.

Rebecca Whitlinger applied everyday creativity with a unique fundraiser featuring once-worn bridesmaid gowns and other "never-to-be-worn again" outfits that netted $90,000 for the Cancer Caring Center between 1998 and 2001 (Flora, 2009).

Another example is using common household items, such as peanut butter and ketchup, to clean the house (Rodgers, 2020). (Yes, ketchup cleans metal, and peanut butter can "unstick" stickers and gum mushed into a carpet.)

Three Steps to Creative Problem-Solving

But how do everyday innovators start out? Where does problem-solving and opportunity-finding begin? The process can be broken down into three simple steps to creative problem-solving: problem-finding, developing a creative question, and taking a problem-solving action. (Note: More detailed and comprehensive CPS models exist. I am speaking broadly.) These steps, some of which may not be done consciously, will help in getting into the minds of our everyday innovators a bit more.

CPS Step 1: Problem-Finding

Each of the stories in this book started with something that many of us try to avoid at all costs: a problem. In creative problem-solving, running *toward* the problem is a start. Roth's (2015) view that life is essentially a "problem-solving activity" makes sense (p. 241), and reframing dilemmas as opportunities transforms problem-solving into gifts…gifts to help us in the "natural development of our life-giving forces" (p. 242).

Being a problem-finder is not necessarily easy. Life problems can be ambiguous, and how a problem is defined or clarified often points to its possible solution (Abdulla et al., 2018). Problem-finding, then, is deemed to be a first step in creative problem-solving that influences steps taken afterward (Reiter-Palmon, 2017), and thus the scholarly work on problem-finding is vast. Abdulla et al. looked at the research on problem-finding from 1960 to 2015 and found a significant correlation between creativity and the finding of challenges. As a person increases in problem-finding, their level of creativity also increases. So, regardless of what it is called—problem discovery or problem identification—there appears to be a link between this skill and creativity. Its importance has been known for a while, too: This idea was also discussed by Alex Osborn, a pioneer in creative thinking in the 1950s.

CPS Step 2: Developing a Creative Question (CQ)

After finding and defining a problem, whether consciously or unconsciously, the people in the case studies asked a question. They developed a creative question (CQ) to guide them in their innovation. Perhaps the question was crystal clear to them from the beginning, or perhaps it evolved over time. Dyer, Gregersen, and Christensen (2011) devoted an entire chapter to the art of questioning as being one of the five key skills for "disruptive innovators," a descriptor found in the subtitle of their book. They pointed out that such innovators could fill a room with thought-provoking questions as catalysts for creativity. After all, questioning helps people better understand the present and the future.

The CQ can guide creative efforts, and how the question is framed is as important as problem-finding itself. The question stem can be prompted by "How might I…?" or "In what ways might we…?" (Creative Education Foundation, 2015). On the other hand, sometimes the question is actually a statement, started by something like, "I wish …" or "It would be great if…" (Miller et al., 2011, p. 63).

Would you like to ask better questions? If so, the invitation is to view the world with a different lens. When doing so, you may just find yourself making observations and finding the right questions in the same spirit as Jonas Salk, the scientist who developed the polio vaccine, who believed that the answers came from the proper questions (Dyer et al., 2011). As you get into the chapters of this book, you'll see that the CQ is identified at the beginning of each story of everyday innovation. With all due respect to the innovators—the stars of the stories—the CQ is only my best after-the-fact guess at the question in their mind.

CPS Step 3: Problem-Solving

What really sets everyday innovators apart is that, after finding a problem and asking a question, they take action. Or, perhaps better stated, they take *actions*. The first attempt at problem-solving may not land in the success column. It's analogous to a principle in design thinking, a solution-focused approach to problem-solving: fail fast. Make a prototype of what might work, try it out, watch the results, tweak the model, and try it out again.

The process echoes the directions on a shampoo bottle: "Rinse and repeat." In problem-solving, however, the repeat cycle offers tweaks to past attempts at success. After all, in the words of Babineaux and Krumboltz, "Success is usually preceded by bumbling starts and botched efforts" (p. 28). Edison was successful in 1,093 patent applications, but another 500–600 submissions were either denied or deserted (Rutgers School of Arts and Sciences, 2016). Problem-solving is not a single-attempt effort. Try, observe, reformulate, and try again.

Taking action on problem-solving can be a complex thing for two reasons. First, there is the work involved. It may not be easy, and it may not be quick. Expert creativity can entail years of dedication, and, by the same token, everyday creativity can take considerable time in understanding a topic and placing a new spin on the job at hand. Otto Rohwedder exemplified incredible dedication and determination over 16 years in toiling on his invention, a device that may affect your life every day. A jeweler by profession, Rohwedder succeeded in perfecting the automatic bread slicer in 1928 despite health difficulties, financial despair, and an absence of interest in his idea (Michalko, 2006). Even after perfecting the slicer, some bakers saw sliced bread as a mere fad, and it took another couple years before such loaves could be found throughout the United States (Nix, 2018). By 1933, 80% of the bread sold was already sliced (Michalko). Without Rohwedder's persistence, what would have been "the greatest thing since sliced bread"?

Second, costs are associated with creative output, as innovators risk rejection and ridicule (Beghetto & Kaufman, 2013). For students, it can be risky to read a story while at the front of the class in the same way that another student takes a chance at being dismissed by a teacher when offering a new perspective on a challenge in math. As Beghetto and Kaufman reminded, "It does not take many such incidents for a student to learn that it's not worth the effort and risk to share personal ideas—it's much easier to provide the answers that teachers and peers expect" (p. 14). Adults who implement their creativity face the same dilemma. The risk factor in expressing and sharing creative ventures takes courage. Resistance to new ideas can be fierce, and many innovative ventures are called "controversial" because they break from the norm. Dr. Andreas Gruentzig performed the first coronary angioplasty procedure in 1977, but the idea of using a balloon catheter was met with skepticism from colleagues when first presented at a conference two years earlier (Emory University School of Medicine, n.d.).

Other examples of discouragement are evident throughout history. Farmers rejected Charles Newbold's idea of a cast-iron plow on the grounds that it would pollute the soil and promote the growth of weeds. Dr. Horace Wells proposed the use of nitrous oxide gas during tooth extractions, but the medical profession scoffed at the idea. Weavers were so threatened by John Kay's invention of a flying shuttle that they destroyed his mold. Altogether, Osborn (1963) reminded, "Most of the greatest ideas were at first greeted with sneers" (p. 54). These examples show one main thing: The problem-solving step involves some risk, including ridicule, damage to one's image, and the discouragement of being shut down or turned away. Problem-solvers accept these risks as a trade-off for the satisfaction of solving a problem. In the well-known words of artist Henri Matisse, "Creativity takes courage."

Before scampering forward, a few summary points may be helpful. In problem-solving, Robert Frost may have been right in his famous poem, "The Road Not Taken." When driving along the Problem Parkway of Life, it's altogether too tempting to stay on the familiar streets where past solutions live. However, the proverbial roads *less traveled* can be the real Solutions Streets of Life. Following them may reveal neighborhoods of innovative ideas. These Solutions Streets are in your GPS; they are not outside of "the box." Even those smaller houses on the Solutions Streets are worth a look, for they may hold the keys to everyday life challenges. And remember: Veering off to unchartered territory can be an enjoyable adventure that takes a degree of courage, persistence, and openness.

Getting to the Edge with SCAMPER

Regardless of the contribution by an innovator, the question at which I continually marvel is, "How did they use their creativity to get this idea?" In essence, how did their problem-solving happen? To dig into this question, we'll use a well-known creativity tool and acronym, SCAMPER. Drawing from its description by creative thinking pioneer Alex Osborn (1963), Eberle (1971) developed a game from the letters that was intended to help youth in their "creative imagination development"

(p. 202). It is an easy and rather enjoyable foundation from which to launch possibilities. Let's look at what each letter of SCAMPER represents.

S: Substitute. Think about Ruth Wakefield, the originator of the chocolate chip cookie in the 1930s, who, according to one story, used "something different" in a butterscotch nut cookie recipe. That *substitution* changed the world of cookies forever when she sprinkled small bits of a semi-sweet chocolate bar into the dough (Roberts, 2018). Wakefield substituted an ingredient, but you can also think about substituting ideas, people, rules, attitudes, or any number of resources.

C: Combine. Charles Spearman, a pioneer in the study of intelligence, proposed that creativity is the outcome of two or more ideas that were previously separate (Balzac, 2006). *Combining* is putting two things together that hadn't previously been together. At one point, for instance, the idea of putting chocolate and peanut butter together would have seemed ludicrous, but this union is now a staple of American desserts and candy. As Henry (2013) wrote, "Each creative idea is the combination of previously existing ideas, or bits of stimuli, into something new" (p. 137).

A: Adapt. Adapting to a new environment or work schedule can offer individuals a different way of being more constructive and productive (Buser et al., 2011). As people age, they *creatively adapt* to different life roles (Gladding, 2016). Talk to any parent and they inevitably tell you that raising children involves some—perhaps a great deal of—creativity. When finding ways to adapt, it can be helpful to examine similar problems in other contexts and consider how others' solutions could play out in your problem-solving.

M: Modify (Magnify or Minimize). Consider how things may be "*modified*" with this part of the acronym. This process could involve making something larger (magnify) or smaller (minimize). It is not just in size, either—it could be in speed, weight, value, or more. The evolution of cars over the past century has been striking. Magnifying them resulted in vans, pickup trucks, campers, and, yes, even hearses, while much smaller compact cars make parallel parking less stressful. A walk-through of any residence finds an assortment of the "M" in windows. From picture windows (magnification) to transom windows (minimization), the idea of inserting glass into a wall can be modified in many creative ways.

P: Put to other uses. A pen is not just used for writing; it can be put to other use as a letter opener, a decoration, or something to prevent a door from entirely closing. Take any item—a mobile phone, a paper clip, a candle—and realize that it could be utilized many ways other than its original intended purpose. After all, George Washington Carver found 300 uses for a peanut (Michalko, 2006). Remember *The Sound of Music* and how Maria, the character played by Julie Andrews, made play clothes out of curtains? That's a creative way to put something to other uses.

E: Eliminate. "Elimination" may not be the first word that a person would choose to associate with creativity, but this process again adds a distinctive flavor in making something different. A food truck, for example, eliminates the building of a restaurant. Meanwhile, a diet where food is removed changes one's intake (Gladding, 2016). Elimination has the added benefit of simplifying or streamlining.

R: Rearrange or Reverse. Mix something in a way that hasn't occurred previously. Place the trunk of a car in the front instead of the back (thank you, Volkswagen Beetle). Eating dessert first is a perfect (and potentially delicious) idea when thinking of "R." Incidentally, while writing this, I learned that Eating Dessert First (EDF) is formally celebrated in late April as a way to help children diagnosed with cancer. (Visit eatdessertfirstday.org to find out more.)

Take any successful venture, and, to some extent, SCAMPER can be applied to better understand the creative problem-solving process. Michalko (2006) examined the history of McDonald's, a global restaurant made famous by Ray Kroc. Kroc had sold paper cups for 17 years before moving to sales of the Multimixer, a device that could make six milkshakes at a time. He noticed six Multimixer orders by a restaurant in 1954. Curious about the restaurant, he looked into it and found a restaurant owned by Dick and Maurice McDonald that had capitalized on the concept of fast food. Kroc and the McDonalds subsequently formed a partnership; Kroc eventually became a billionaire, but only through weathering challenges that reflected SCAMPER.

Michalko cited examples in modifying (magnifying) a hamburger into the Big Mac and changing the way that french fries were made. Kroc also applied the "put to other uses" strategy by leasing a site, then developing it, and finally re-leasing it to a franchisee. Another example? Consider the "C" of combination in the creation of the Happy Meal. (Incidentally, if you were also guessing that McDonald's applied the "substitute" by adding a drive-through option, you would be incorrect. This honor goes to Red's Giant Hamburg in Springfield, Missouri, in 1947 (Tuttle, 2014).)

To review, the brain may be stumped sometimes in a narrow thinking mode—it may be utilizing only the middle "safe areas" of the playing field rather than approaching the boundaries. People solving problems in creative ways did three things: a) identified a problem, b) asked a creative question, and c) problem-solved, in one way or another. The seven letters of SCAMPER identified by Eberle help people during the last step, as they work to develop ideas that are within reach (in the box), but perhaps not quickly imagined (on the edges).

A Few Pointers

I want to share a few final gems before getting to the case studies. The first is about the word that our parents told us never to do. Remember that phrase about assumptions: "Never assume because it makes…," yes, you remember the rest. Assumptions are dangerous, yet in many ways inevitable. In creativity, go sideways with assumptions by developing awareness of them. Make them, take them, and then question them. Creativity expert Michael Michalko wrote, "Problems are often salted with assumptions that hinder creativity" (2006, p. 45). According to him, challenging assumptions is critical in problem-solving. After all, he added, "any assumption can be challenged," and even Edison, a great innovator, sought people who regularly questioned assumptions.

How does one challenge assumptions? Reverse them. Let's try it. Assume that restaurants must have menus. Now, challenge that assumption: What if some restaurants didn't have menus? What would that look like? How would the restaurant work? Suddenly, possibilities open up that weren't there before. The beauty of challenging assumptions is the result: It disrupts traditional patterns of thought and enables information to be put together in exciting unique ways (Michalko). During my college days and prior to basketball's shot clock being introduced, I witnessed a brilliant execution of rejecting assumptions. My school's basketball team rejected the assumption of the speed at which basketball games are normally played. A big game was coming up and we anticipated a loss to a team with superior talent, but our coach had a plan. He slooooowed the pace of the entire 40 minutes. It became a remarkably low-scoring game, yet a victory (30–29) nonetheless. Remember how everyday creativity happens at the edges of the box or the edge of the court? Utilizing these edges and boundaries by rejecting assumptions opens up the playing space and provides more room for ideas to work.

Additionally, as you read the stories in the upcoming chapters, I invite you to marvel at their creative simplicity. Creative problem-solving can be deceptively and yet brilliantly simple: In how many ways can a cup be made? Well, of course the answer is dozens of ways: cupping one's hands, using a ladle, and emptying a container of yogurt, to name a few. Now I invite you to go back in time about 100,000 years to southern Africa. People used ostrich eggs as water bottles (Barras, 2014). Again creativity, whether in the 2020s or 100,000 years ago, can be magnificently small.

I leave you with a fascinating, mesmerizing quote: "The truth is, your mind contains a near-infinite number of ideas and memories that at any given moment are lurking outside your consciousness" (Johnson, 2010, p. 110). The innovators in the stories ahead don't necessarily have more advanced brains. They simply tapped into those lurkers and implemented them. They didn't let themselves get trapped on an unmoving escalator. They started simply by finding a problem and asking a question. Now, let's dive in.

Sources

Abdulla, A. M., Paek, S. H., Cramond, B., & Runco, M. A. (2018). Problem finding and creativity: A meta-analytic review. *Psychology of Aesthetics, Creativity, and the Arts 14*(1), 3–14. https://doi.org/10.1037/aca0000194

Babineaux, R., & Krumboltz, J. (2013). *Fail fast, fail often: How losing can help you win.* Jeremy P. Tarcher/Penguin.

Balzac, F. (2006, May). Exploring the brain's role in creativity. *NeuroPsychiatry Reviews, 7*(5), pp. 1, 19–20.

Barras, C. (2014, October 25). Transformers. *NewScientist*, pp. 32–36.

Beghetto, R. A. (2013). *Killing ideas softly? The promise and perils of creativity in the classroom*. Information Age Publishing, Inc.

Beghetto, R. A., & Kaufman, J. C. (2013). Fundamentals of creativity. *Educational Leadership, 70*(5), 10–15.

Buser, J., Buser, T., Gladding, S., & Wilkerson, J. (2011). The creative counselor: Using the SCAMPER model in counselor training. *Journal of Creativity in Mental Health, 6*(4), 256–273. https://doi.org/10.1080/15401383.2011.631468

Creative Education Foundation. (2015). *Educating for creativity level 1 resource guide*. http://www.creativeeducationfoundation.org/wp-content/uploads/2015/06/EFC-Level-1-FINALelectronic.pdf

Dyer, J., & Gregersen, H. (2011, September 27). Learn how to think different(ly). *Harvard Business Review*. https://hbr.org/2011/09/begin-to-think-differently

Dyer, J., Gregersen, H., & Christensen, C. M. (2011). *The innovator's DNA: Mastering the five skills of disruptive innovators*. Harvard Business Review Press.

Eberle, R. F. (1971). *SCAMPER: Games for imagination development*. DOK Publishers, Inc.

Eberle, R. F. (1972). Developing imagination through scamper. *Journal of Creative Behavior, 6*(3), 199–203.

Emory University School of Medicine. (n.d.). *The first balloon angioplasty procedure on a coronary artery*. https://med.emory.edu/gamechangers/researchers/gruentzig/bio.html

Flora, C. (2009, November 1). *Everyday creativity*. Psychology Today. https://www.psychologytoday.com/us/articles/200911/everyday-creativity

Gladding, S. T. (2016). *The creative arts in counseling* (5th ed.). American Counseling Association.

Gladding, S. T., & Wallace, M. J. D. (2010). The potency and power of counseling stories. *Journal of Creativity in Mental Health, 5*(1), 15–24. https://doi.org/10.1080/15401381003640569

Heath, C., & Heath, D. (2007). *Made to stick: Why some ideas survive and others die*. Random House.

Henry, T. (2013). *The accidental creative: How to be brilliant at a moment's notice*. Portfolio/Penguin.

Johnson, S. (2010). *Where good ideas come from*. Riverhead Books.

Kaufman, J. C. (2016). *Creativity 101* (2nd ed.). Springer Publishing Company

Kaufman, J. C., & Beghetto, R. A. (2009). Beyond big and little: The Four C model of creativity. *Review of General Psychology, 13*(1), 1–12.

Kaufman, S. B. (Host). (2019, April 18). Everyday creativity with Ruth Richards (No. 162) [Audio podcast episode]. In *The Psychology Podcast*. https://scottbarrykaufman.com/podcast/everyday-creativity-with-ruth-richards/

Kida, T. (2006). *Don't believe everything you think: The 6 basic mistakes we make in thinking*. Prometheus Books.

King, S. R. (1998, September 10). Juan Metzer, 79, is dead: He put the fruit in yogurt. *The New York Times*. https://www.nytimes.com/1998/09/10/business/juan-metzger-79-is-dead-he-put-the-fruit-in-yogurt.html

Linkner, J. (2011). *Disciplined dreaming: A proven system to drive breakthrough creativity*. Jossey-Bass.

Madson, P. R. (2005). *Improv wisdom: Don't prepare, just show up*. Bell Tower.

Michalko, M. (2006). *Thinkertoys: A handbook of creative-thinking techniques* (2nd ed.). Ten Speed Press.

Miller, B., Vehar, J., Firestien, R., Thurber, S., & Nielsen, D. (2011). *Creativity unbound* (5th ed.). Creative Education Foundation.

Nix, E. (2018, August 22). *Who invented sliced bread?* History. https://www.history.com/news/who-invented-sliced-bread

Noller, R. B. (1979). *Scratching the surface of creative problem-solving: A bird's eye view of CPS*. DOK.

Osborn, A. F. (1963). *Applied imagination* (3rd revised ed.). Charles Scribner's Sons.

Reiter-Palmon, R. (2017). The role of problem construction in creative production. *Journal of Creative Behavior, 51*(4), 323–326. https://doi.org/10.1002/jocb.202

Richards, R. (2007). Everyday creativity: Our hidden potential. In R. Richards (Ed.), *Everyday creativity and new views of human nature: Psychological, social, and spiritual perspectives* (pp. 25–53). American Psychological Association. https://doi.org/10.1037/11595-001

Roberts, S. (2018, March 21). Overlooked no more: Ruth Wakefield, who invented the chocolate chip cookie. *The New York Times*. https://www.nytimes.com/2018/03/21/obituaries/overlooked-ruth-wakefield.html

Rodgers, M. (2020, January 19). *10 foods that can substitute as cleaning supplies*. TribLive. https://triblive.com/lifestyles/10-foods-that-can-substitute-as-cleaning-supplies/

Roth, B. (2015). *The achievement habit: Stop wishing, start doing, and take command of your life*. HarperCollins.

Rutgers School of Arts and Sciences. (2016, October 28). *Thomas A. Edison papers*. https://edison.rutgers.edu/patents.htm

Seelig, T. (2015). *Creativity rules: Get ideas out of your head and into the world.* Harper One.

Tuttle, B. (2014, October 8). 10 things you didn't know about the fast food drive-thru. *Money.* https://money.com/drive-thru-fast-food-fast-casual/

Walker, R. (2019). *The art of noticing: 131 ways to spark creativity, find inspiration, and discover joy in the everyday.* Alfred A. Knopf.

Chapter 1

Let's Look at Creativity Questions

Before we dive in, here's an overview of what to expect in the 50 chapters ahead. Each chapter briefly highlights one or more everyday innovations and connects the innovators' efforts within the SCAMPER framework (see the Introduction). I've tried to get inside the head of each everyday innovator and take a guess at the Creative Question (CQ) they were grappling with. Remember, the innovator doesn't have to formally ask or write down their CQ, but the CQ listed is my best guess at one of the questions or ideas that may have sparked their innovation.

Here are a few reminders of key acronyms from the Introduction that you'll see throughout the rest of this book:

CPS: Creative Problem-Solving

CQ: Creative Question

SCAMPER

S: Substitute

C: Combine

A: Adapt

M: Modify

P: Put to Other Uses

E: Eliminate

R: Rearrange or Reverse

Chapter 2

CQ: What Can Fill a Hole?

CPS: Pavement fatigue—yes, pavement fatigue—can be a top reason for potholes, particularly through aging, as pavement loses flexibility from continuous traffic and weather conditions. Improper drainage can also contribute. Potholes are a menace to drivers, especially when they are difficult to see. If you think your town or city is the worst for potholes, think again. One person in India nominated Mumbai to be entered in the *Guinness Book of World Records* for its pothole infamy of an estimated 20,000 such roadway obstacles.

The question, then, is how to creatively repair potholes. Two innovative approaches have been used in recent years. First, to the surprise of some residents, Littleton, Colorado, used tar combined with single-ply toilet paper, which absorbs oil from the tar and prevents it from getting on cars. The paper is biodegradable, disappearing in days. Repairs are kept to a minimum in terms of time. Incidentally, Littleton officials had learned from another city that used the same trick in fixing potholes. Lincoln, Nebraska, also used toilet paper, though it was a two-ply tissue where the upper ply wasn't absorbent, resulting in it blowing into residents' yards.

A second approach is Domino's "Paving for Pizza" campaign, which started in 2018 with a mission toward "pizzas getting back to their home safely," according to the company's director of PR. In collaboration with four towns in the United States during its initial phase, Domino's offered a paving grant that included Domino's stencils for the repaired potholes, stickers for the equipment, signs to use during the paving, and a gift card for the work crew. During the first week alone, "Paving for Pizza" ignited 35,000 organic mentions on social media.

SCAMPER code: Substitute. Substituting items not usually seen in pothole repair can be successful, especially when you're hungry.

Question for creative thought: I once read a story where a town found tourists speeding through the downtown area. After exploring potential solutions, they arrived on something creative: implanting fake potholes in the road. Whether you're making or filling potholes, roads are critical to our journeys. What creative ways can you make your road bumpier or smoother to meet your needs?

Sources

Aguilar, J. (2016, November 4). Littleton TP's its own streets as a way to fill its cracks—single-ply only. *The Denver Post*. https://www.denverpost.com/2016/11/03/littleton-tps-its-own-streets-as-a-way-to-fill-its-cracks-single-ply-only/

Asphalt Pavement Solutions. (n.d.). *What causes potholes?* https://asphaltpavementsolutions.com/what-causes-potholes

Moneycontrol News. (2018, July 24). *Mumbai to be in Guinness and Limca books of world records for potholes?* https://www.moneycontrol.com/news/india/mumbai-to-be-in-guinness-and-limca-books-of-world-records-for-potholes-2752851.html

Wolfson, S. (2018, June 12). *Domino's branded potholes appear after pizza company takes to road repair.* The Guardian. https://www.theguardian.com/business/2018/jun/12/dominos-pizza-deliveries-road-repair-potholes-paving-infrastructure

Chapter 3

CQ: How Can Passengers Move Through Airports More Efficiently?

CPS: Bernard Sadow called this idea from 1970 one of his best ever. In returning from a vacation in Aruba, he lugged two heavy suitcases to the customs line at the airport. While waiting, he noticed a heavy machine moving along on a skid with wheels. He looked at his wife and commented, "You know, that's what we need for luggage." As a vice president of a company that manufactured luggage and coats, he was already familiar with suitcases. He set to work on a prototype, taking casters from a wardrobe trunk and placing them on a large suitcase. "I put a strap on the front and pulled it, and it worked," he said.

Patent No. 3,653,474 ensued in 1972, though success was not automatic. Sadow spent months in sales calls to large department stores and didn't fare well. The reason? Men wouldn't be interested in suitcases with wheels, or so he was told. Sadow called it a "very macho thing," adding that people simply do not meet change very well.

In 1987, pilot Robert Plath modified the suitcase idea and developed the Rollaboard. His idea resulted in a two-wheeled, long-handled suitcase that he initially sold only to other crew members. Airline passengers subsequently saw the ease in moving luggage, and Plath left the cockpit to start a company born on the invention.

Now, 50 years later, it's difficult—perhaps impossible—to find a suitcase without wheels

SCAMPER code: Substitute. Mr. Sadow found a way to change travel by simply substituting a machine part into an everyday item. (Note: If there were cell phones in 1970, he may have been looking at his phone while waiting in line. Would the wheeled suitcase have ever been developed?)

Question for creative thought: The suitcase continues to evolve since Mr. Sadow's patent was filed. Different locks have been made. Newer materials are being used. Built-in batteries for charging electronic devices are much more common. What other features can you imagine to improve this all-important travel item?

Source

Sharkey, J. (2010, October 4). Reinventing the suitcase by adding the wheel. *The New York Times*. https://www.nytimes.com/2010/10/05/business/05road.html

Chapter 4

CQ: How Can I Help Others See a New Perspective?

CPS: With mobile phones becoming instant cameras, the interest in the disposable camera has likely dipped over the years. Not for Café Art, though—this London group uses art, photography, and entrepreneurship to empower individuals affected by homelessness. After offering photography training through the Royal Photographic Society, Café Art gave 100 disposable cameras to individuals who were homeless. The participants were asked to take pictures around the theme of "My London."

Each camera offered 27 photo opportunities to capture London from new perspectives, and, since 2012, Café Art has been using these images in a yearly calendar. Profits from the project are reinvested to cover printing, art supplies, photography training, and payments for the photographers.

Perhaps most importantly, the project combats stigma around homeless populations with the notion that increased empathy results from seeing others' perspectives. By offering people affected by homelessness with this outlet, Café Art is able to "connect them to a world in which they might not feel welcome."

SCAMPER code: Combine. The motto on the webpage says it all: "Where homelessness, great art & coffee meet." Information about this year's calendar can be found there as well.

Question for creative thought: If I gave you a disposable camera with capacity for only 12 photos, what important images would you capture and why?

Sources

Café Art. (n.d.). https://www.cafeart.org.uk/

Molloy, P. (2015, August 31). *What happens when you give 100 homeless people disposable cameras? True works of art*. Upworthy. https://www.upworthy.com/what-happens-when-you-give-100-homeless-people-disposable-cameras-true-works-of-art

Chapter 5

CQ: Can Urine Help People Who Are Refugees?

CPS: Professor Ioannis Ieropoulos's interest in microbial fuel cells (MFCs) sparked an idea: If, as the University of the West of England professor found, urine could power a phone, then could it also supply the electricity in a place such as a refugee camp? In 2015, the University partnered with Oxfam, a social services organization that works globally, on this possibility. Designed to resemble the toilet facilities in a refugee camp, a prototype urinal was installed near the bar in the Student Union. An official with Oxfam called the technology "a huge step forward" that had significant potential.

The added benefit is one of cost. An MFC cell is relatively inexpensive, costing around US $1.50. Professor Ieropoulos estimated that a small unit similar to the prototype could cost around US $600, which is an important consideration given that the technology is theoretically everlasting.

Other applications? A 2019 video by the Australian Broadcasting Corporation discusses the Urinotron, a device able to generate enough power to recharge a mobile phone using urine. Professor Peter Scales, a University of Melbourne faculty member and one of the project collaborators, is shown describing the process behind the device to school students on a city street through a visual display on "Reimagining your Waste." In addition to prompting dialogues, the display makes people think, according to Tilly Boleyn, the gallery curator. In her experience, the conversation begins with something to the effect of "This is disgusting…I do not want to do it" and transforms to "Yeah, this is something that we should think about" after interacting with the display. The change in perspectives, she added, is "an absolute joy to behold."

SCAMPER code: Combine. Bringing together MFCs and urine to produce electricity could have a sustainable impact for a population that would greatly benefit.

Question for creative thought: What everyday item in your world could be applied to a community problem in an innovative way?

Sources

ABC News. (2019, August 19). *Pee power: Recharge your mobile phone with urine* [video]. https://www.youtube.com/watch?v=buJhuJIACx0

Tully, A. (2015, March 14). *'Pee power': A new way to light up refugee camps.* Time. https://time.com/3744396/urinals-power-refugee-camps/

Chapter 6

CQ: What Happens to Those Crayons that Came with Dinner?

CPS: Crayola Crayons were offered in two colors when they were first made in 1864: charcoal and lampblack. By today's standards, they wouldn't be considered the most imaginative of colors, particularly when compared to such current shades as "Purple Pizzazz," "Gel FX Magenta," and "Outer Space." Availability isn't necessarily a problem, either, since Crayola churns out three billion crayons per year. (That translates to twelve million crayons per day, if you're interested.)

Whether they are officially Crayola or otherwise, servers at kid-friendly restaurants often bring a small packet of crayons to customers with children. After all, it's a brilliant way to keep them occupied before the food is served. But, after that, what happens to the used—and unused—crayons? Bryan Ware had the same question while dining at a restaurant with his wife and two boys.

He subsequently discovered two things: 1) The crayons were typically single-use and found their way to garbage dumps after the restaurant; and 2) Crayons are not environmentally friendly. In fact, over 500,000 pounds of crayons are thrown out yearly. As a result, he developed The Crayon Initiative, an effort to collect crayons from restaurants and beyond (schools and homes, too) for recycling and reuse. The crayons are melted down and then remanufactured. As the initiative's website says, "That's what we call thinking outside the Crayon Box."

The Crayon Initiative has collected over 41 million crayons and delivered crayons to over 430,000 children in hospitals throughout the country, aiding their art programs and helping children with their creative processes. Interested in learning more? Visit thecrayoninitiative.org.

SCAMPER code: Adapt. By collecting the used and unused crayons from restaurants and adapting them in a new setting, Ware and The Crayon Initiative have found another way that crayons can be enjoyed.

Question for creative thought: I invite you to do something that you may not have done for years: Get a box of crayons and a blank piece of paper. Set a timer for five minutes and color whatever comes to mind…something, anything. What ideas, big or small, came to mind during your five minutes?

Sources

Crayola. (n.d.). *Explore colors*. https://www.crayola.com/explore-colors/

Crayola. (n.d.). *How many Crayola products do you make per year?* https://www.crayola.com/faq/your-business/how-many-crayola-products-do-you-make-per-year/

Molloy, P. (2015, September 9). *What happens to restaurant crayons? This dad found and decided to do something about it.* Upworthy. https://www.upworthy.com/what-happens-to-restaurant-crayons-this-dad-found-out-and-decided-to-do-something-about-it?u=04b58c77b3b3509ea4c4e1d4ce752dc0720bfd6d

Rodell, C. (2013). *Use all the crayons! The colorful guide to simple human happiness.* iUniverse.

The Crayon Mission. (n.d.). *Our mission*. https://thecrayoninitiative.org/about/

The Crayon Mission. (n.d.). *Who we are*. https://thecrayoninitiative.org/

Chapter 7

CQ: How Could a Suicide Attempt Be Prevented?

CPS: Midnight had passed for drivers on Interstate 696 in Detroit on a Tuesday morning in April, but, less than an hour later, the situation changed drastically. A man was threatening to attempt suicide by jumping from one of the freeway overpasses. Michigan State Police halted traffic in the six lanes leading in both directions, an initial step that attempts to calm someone contemplating suicide.

The subsequent action entailed drivers' help, specifically those driving semitrucks. The state troopers began calling drivers in the area to assist by forming a line below the bridge to deter the man from jumping from the overpass. "It provides a safety net for the person in case they happen to lose their grip and fall or if they decide to jump," noted Lt. Mike Shaw, a spokesperson for the Michigan State Police. "With the trucks lined up underneath they're only falling about five or six feet as opposed [to] 15 or 16."

About two hours later, the man threatening suicide stepped down. Police posted a photo of the "truck wall," made possible by caring semitruck drivers, on Twitter.

SCAMPER code: Put to other uses. The top of a semitruck can be used as a roof for the contents of a truck as well as, in this case, a landing place…and hopefully a safe one at that.

Question for creative thought: Bridges are magnificent structures that carry us from one place to the next. What bridges have you successfully crossed in life and who have been "safety nets" in assisting you?

Source

Romo, V. (2018, April 24). *Truckers line up under bridge to save man threatening suicide*. NPR. https://www.npr.org/sections/thetwo-way/2018/04/24/605353976/truckers-line-up-under-bridge-to-save-man-threatening-suicide

Chapter 8

CQ: How Can Tourists Be Attracted to a Place 200 Kilometers North of the Arctic Circle?

CPS: When you hear the word "hotel," what comes to mind? A building with a lobby, perhaps a restaurant and a pool, and multiple floors of guestrooms? A trip to Jukkasjärvi, a town of 548 people in northern Sweden, would likely result in seeing a church built around 1607, but the real attraction is only about 30 years old: a hotel made of ice, aptly named Icehotel.

And to think that it started with a simple question. The hotel evolved from an art gallery of ice sculptures, which was originally sparked by the success of an ice sculpting workshop. ARTic Hall grew over time, gaining increased attention, to the point where a group of people asked if they could stay overnight within the confines of the icy structure. Thus, Icehotel was started.

Icehotel is re-created each November by a group of 40 creative artists who bring their talents and designs to complete the facility in about six weeks. It features 120 rooms, about 50 of which are designated as "cold" rooms that eventually melt back into the local river when the weather warms. The average temperature in the "cold" rooms is about 17–23 degrees Fahrenheit, and guests are offered a morning sauna to start the day. Since the hotel started as a gallery, art continues to be a theme of the Icehotel. Each room is carefully and uniquely sculpted, and ice masterpieces adorn rooms throughout the attraction.

SCAMPER code: Modify. Icehotel has modified the typical guest experience as it takes on a different feel (not to mention temperature) through ice.

Questions for creative thought: Whether you enjoy or detest cold environments, how would an evening or two in a hotel like this awaken your observation? What would you notice from your experience that would relate to your creative thinking?

Sources

Visit Sweden. (n.d.). *Celebrating 30 years of Icehotel, the coolest hotel in the world.* https://visitsweden.com/icehotel/

Jukkasjärvi. (n.d.). Wikipedia. https://en.wikipedia.org/wiki/Jukkasj%C3%A4rvi

Chapter 9

CQ: How Might I Find a Product to Sell that I Believe In?

CPS: The title of Bill O'Hanlon's 1999 book says it all: *Do One Thing Different: Ten Simple Ways to Change Your Life*. This title is reminiscent of the phrase about repetition and problem-solving mentioned in the Introduction: Insanity is doing the same over and over and expecting a different result. O'Hanlon asks problem-solvers to take a different approach. He challenges them to alter the *"doing" of the problem* by breaking the *pattern of the problem*. After all, new actions could result in new feelings, and, when it comes to creativity, new outcomes.

Consider Spanx, a clothing line created by Sara Blakely. After deciding that law school was not for her given her LSAT results, she worked at Disney World for three months before getting a cold-call sales position for fax machines. Most sales calls ended in failure; she described getting doors slammed in her face and her business cards being ripped up in front of her. Nonetheless, she developed increased confidence in her ability to sell, and seven years into the fax machine chapter of her career, she visualized being self-employed with her own business.

She then described one thing she did differently: "In the hopes of looking better in my fitted white pants, I cut the feet out of a pair of pantyhose and substituted them for my underwear." (Did you hear the SCAMPER word in that quote?) The single change ignited an idea: Why not create an innovative kind of body shapewear? The idea, she added, was the outcome of what she had been mentally laying the foundation for during this time in her life. At one point, Forbes estimated her net worth at over $1.1 billion, all due to doing one thing differently.

SCAMPER code: Substitution. A small change led to huge success.

Question for creative thought: With O'Hanlon's quote in mind, is there a *doing of the problem* in your life that could be altered?

Sources

O'Hanlon, B. (1999). *Do one thing different.* William Morrow and Company, Inc. See p. 8 to reference "doing the problem."

Segal, G. Z. (2015). *Getting there: A book of mentors.* Abrams Image. See p. 34.

Schwantes, M. (2018, September 25). *Spanx founder Sara Blakely just identified the no. 1 reason why people don't succeed (and it's quite brilliant).* Inc. https://www.inc.com/marcel-schwantes/spanx-founder-sara-blakely-just-identified-no-1-reason-why-people-dont-succeed-and-its-quite-brilliant.html

Chapter 10

CQ: How Can More People Become Interested in Sweden?

CPS: Perhaps you've never visited Sweden, a country of about 10 million in northern Europe. Sweden has a lot going for it. It is #3 in the world in exporting music (behind the U.S. and U.K.). The country actually imports garbage, given its efficiency in waste-handling and recycling, and it is first in the world in offering foreign aid (1.41% of its gross national income). Sweden also ranked as the seventh most creative country in the world, according to the Global Creative Index 2015.

To help others learn more about the country, a tourism agency had an idea: Why not give people outside Sweden the chance to call a resident and just talk? The hope is to give non-Swedes a more authentic perspective of the nation and its culture. About 3,000 Swedes volunteered to be phone ambassadors by merely downloading an app. They included, for example, a 28-year-old woman working in marketing, a 38-year-old man in communications, and a 21-year-old engineering student. As of April 2016, most of the 7,500 calls came from the United States and Turkey.

One of a Swedish college student's conversations came during his studies for an upcoming test and included the topic of Swedish meatballs. No, he told the caller, "they are generally not made like the ones you eat at Ikea." That's just another thing to know about Sweden . . .

SCAMPER code: Modify. The tourism agency in Sweden modified the information process, making it easier, more enjoyable, and highly engaging.

Question for creative thought: How can people engage with you or your business in a more creative way?

Sources

Florida, R., Mellander, C., & King, K. M. (2015, July 8). *The Global Creativity Index 2015*. http://martinprosperity.org/content/the-global-creativity-index-2015/

Nag, O. S. (2019, August 15). *10 interesting facts about Sweden*. World Atlas. https://www.worldatlas.com/articles/top-10-interesting-facts-about-sweden.html

Victor, D. (2016, April 8). 'Calling Sweden. You will soon be connected to a random Swede, somewhere in Sweden.' *The New York Times*. https://www.nytimes.com/2016/04/09/world/europe/sweden-call-random-swede-number.html

Chapter 11

CQ: How Does a Pinecone Relate to Reading?

CPS: It was an accident. Louis, a 9-year-old boy in France, was helping his father make harnesses for horses when he blinded himself with a hole puncher. The year was 1818. While sitting in his yard a few years later and thinking about his inability to read, a friend serendipitously handed Louis a pinecone. He studied it by touch, noticing the differences in the scales. In doing so, he came to realize that a system of reading and writing could be created so that individuals who are blind could read and write via raised dots on paper. Louis Braille developed new avenues of learning and communication for those with visual difficulties. His tactile connection changed the world for millions of people since then.

More recently, another individual moved to the edge of the box by helping blind animals. Dorie Stratton's realization involved helping animals, specifically her dog named "Scotty Boy," with visual impairments. She brought Scotty Boy home after finding him abandoned in a Walmart parking lot. The dog repeatedly bumped into the wall, similar to how her friend's blind dog had before he passed away. Having no experience with blind dogs, Stratton scoured the internet for ideas and found little helpful information. She then created a halo apparatus to prevent such accidents, and, along with her friend, designed a vest with a ring to help Scotty Boy orient himself in the world. The "Halo Vest" sparked the creation of her company, Halo for Paws, to aid blind animals. Stratton and her friend never intended to become entrepreneurs with their Halo Vests, which have also been designed for cats and sheep with vision problems.

SCAMPER code: Combine. Both Braille and Stratton discovered a problem and used combinations of things in everyday life to address the problem of blindness in people and animals.

Question for creative thought: I invite you to go to a different room in your home or office and pick up an object that you usually wouldn't notice. What other uses could it have in helping you to enhance your life?

Sources

Alignable. (n.d.). Halos for paws. https://www.alignable.com/blairsville-ga/halos-for-paws

Michalko, M. (2011). *Creative thinkering*. New World Library.

Newsner. (2016, May 18). *Her clever invention gives blind animals a new life*. https://en.newsner.com/animals/her-clever-invention-gives-blind-animals-a-new-life/

Chapter 12

CQ: Does Driving in the Rain Have to Be So Risky?

CPS: The car has undergone monumental changes since two bicycle mechanics, J. Frank and Charles Duryea of Springfield, Massachusetts, first designed a gas-powered automobile in the United States in 1893. A few years later the first speeding ticket was issued in England, when driver Walter Arnold was fined for reaching 8 miles per hour in a time when speed limits were 2 mile per hour. The police officer also found that Mr. Arnold's car was not preceded by a man walking and waving a red flag, which was something required for all cars at the time.

Along with advances in speed capabilities, cars have evolved since the 1890s in numerous ways: They come equipped with a defroster, a heater, air conditioning, power steering, heated seats, GPS, headlights, and glove compartments, just to name a few changes. Yet a relatively simple invention revolutionized driving, created by someone not permitted to drive in the first place.

Mary Anderson of Birmingham, Alabama, was visiting New York City in 1903 when she noticed her streetcar driver having to get out of the car to clear snow from the windscreen. Other drivers had to do the same. Car passengers got colder every time the door was opened. After experiencing this dilemma, she worked on a device where the automobile driver could move a rubber blade on the windscreen from *inside* the car. She patented the invention, only to find others skeptical of it. After all, they reasoned, this wiper would distract the driver. One rejection letter noted that her idea lacked any value. Over time, acceptance grew, and the windshield wiper became a critical part of the automobile. Despite Anderson's contribution, she never made any money from her invention, but was posthumously honored with a 2011 induction into the National Inventors Hall of Fame.

SCAMPER code: Modify. Or, perhaps better phrased, modify, modify, modify, and modify again—the evolution of the car has required significant modifications over time. Mary Anderson's wipers were modified further by Bob Kearns, who invented the intermittent wiper. It was an even greater success than his earlier invention of a comb that dispensed tonic.

Question for creative thought: Review the inductees in the National Inventors Hall of Fame (https://www.invent.org/NIHF-hall-of-fame-inductees-list-alphabetical). What other inventions fascinate you, and how might the inventors' thinking help you?

Sources

BBC News. (2017, September 4). *BBC 100 women: Nine things you didn't know were invented by women.* https://www.bbc.com/news/world-40923649

History.com Editors. (2018, August 21). *Automobile history.* https://www.history.com/topics/inventions/automobiles

Karr, A. (2017, May 11). *This is the first car to ever receive a speeding ticket.* motor1.com. https://www.motor1.com/news/145180/first-car-speed-ticket/

Mlodinow, L. (2018). *Elastic: Flexible thinking in a time of change.* Pantheon Books.

Palca, J. (2017, July 25). *Alabama woman stuck in NYC traffic in 1902 invented the windshield wiper.* NPR. https://www.npr.org/2017/07/25/536835744/alabama-woman-stuck-in-nyc-traffic-in-1902-invented-the-windshield-wiper

Vyas, K. (2019, January 25). *24 inventions by women you might not be aware of.* Interesting Engineering. https://amp.interestingengineering.com/24-inventions-by-women-you-might-not-be-aware-of

Chapter 13

CQ: How Might the Frequency of Alcohol Addiction Be Decreased?

CPS: Sometimes being counterintuitive runs parallel to creative problem-solving. This notion holds true in one treatment for alcohol use disorder, a condition marked by symptoms that can include craving it, using it recurrently in physically hazardous situations, and a need for more alcohol to reach the intended effect. Alcohol use disorder affects about 15 million American adults, an estimated 6.2% of the United States population as of 2015.

One approach in helping individuals with alcohol use is harm reduction. The difference between this model compared to abstinence (no use at all) is how progress is defined. In harm reduction, it would be considered a success if a person went from drinking 10 drinks daily to five drinks each day. In other words, drinking less would be seen as "steps in the right direction."

Pressly wrote about one program in Canada where clients with alcohol problems are aided in harm reduction behaviors. The program, entitled the Managed Alcohol Program (MAP), was created for homeless individuals in 2001. Participants line up for the first glass of wine (about seven ounces) at 7:30 a.m. and are subsequently offered five ounces until 9:30 p.m. Any clients displaying signs of intoxication are not served. The harm reduction approach is not without challenge for its staff. One physician—and one of the designers of MAP—said that the hope was to "stabilize the craziness" of the lives of the population they serve. If their day starts with a hunt for alcohol and the ensuing consequences, then perhaps MAP could aid with their mental health, their addictions, and their physical illnesses. Though hard data on the programmatic effectiveness was not available, the physician noted a sharp decrease in related 911 calls. One client who had drank mouthwash and hairspray on the streets said that all she wanted was the effect, adding, "I drink much less here."

SCAMPER code: Substitute. In helping participants go from mouthwash to wine, the creators of MAP are providing a substitute for harmful behavior.

Question for creative thought: Consider the volume button on some sort of device. Can lowering the volume, akin to MAP, possibly aid a problem-opportunity?

Sources

American Psychiatric Association. (2013). *Diagnostic and statistical manual of mental disorders* (5th ed.). https://doi.org/10.1176/appi.books.9780890425596

Logan, D. E., & Marlatt, G. A. (2010). Harm reduction therapy: A practice-friendly review of research. *Journal of Clinical Psychology*, *66*(2), 201–214. https://doi.org/10.1002/jclp.20669

National Institute on Alcohol Abuse and Alcoholism. (n.d.). *Alcohol use disorder*. https://www.niaaa.nih.gov/alcohol-health/overview-alcohol-consumption/alcohol-use-disorders

Pressly, L. (2016, July 7). *Treating alcoholics – with wine*. BBC News. https://www.bbc.com/news/magazine-36717557

Chapter 14

CQ: How Can Airlines Get Passengers' Attention in Flight?

CPS: All of us have "seen" them, but perhaps not really watched them. While the plane makes its way from the gate to the runway, the essential blah-blah-blah of the safety announcements are made in one way or another. Some airline executives, however, had a different idea: Why not make those videos creative…and funny? The chief executive of British Airways said in a statement, "It's extremely important to us that customers engage with our safety video."

"Engaging" seems to be the relevant word, as getting passenger focus away from phones and toward the monitor is paramount. Other airlines, from Virgin America to Air New Zealand to Delta to American, have joined in the humorous openings. After passengers have endured airport traffic, security screenings, prolonged pre-board waits, and struggles with overhead compartments, a few chuckles from passengers is a way to lighten the mood on a flight.

The brief videos have certainly had their share of innovation. Virgin America started the trend in 2007 with an animated clip before moving to videos involving breakdancing nuns. Air New Zealand videos have featured celebrities such as Betty White and Richard Simmons. A Delta flight attendant become known—or "no-known"—as "Deltalina" for her clear gesture about smoking being prohibited. Finally, British Airways teamed with noted actors and comedians in a 2017 video that also raised money for a charity.

While passenger interest is a primary benefit, the safety videos have garnered attention from potential customers viewing them online. Jodi Williams, the Head of Global Brand Development at Air New

Zealand, said that the concept has exceeded expectations, adding, "It took off way better than anyone assumed it would." Whether the pun was intended is unknown.

SCAMPER code: Adapt. Switching up a common routine during a common process sparked attention and smiles.

Question for creative thought: Take conscious energy to really listen to and watch the safety video or demonstration during your next flight. How are the important messages being communicated, and could they be done in a more attention-capturing manner?

Sources

Baillie, R. (2016, August 18). *Reinventing the airline safety speech*. BBC Autos. http://www.bbc.com/autos/story/20160818-reinventing-the-airline-safety-speech

Salic, J. (2017, July 19). 5 flight safety videos worth watching. *The New York Times*. https://www.nytimes.com/2017/07/19/travel/british-airways-flight-safety-videos.html

Chapter 15

CQ: How Might Entrepreneurial Skills Be Taught?

CPS: Dr. Tina Seelig, a Stanford University faculty member who teaches and has written widely on creativity and innovation, believes that entrepreneurial skills are critical to success. She wrote, "It's a crime not to teach young people to be entrepreneurial" (2015, p. 3). After all, she reasoned, college graduates should leave with their degree and a sense of agency, a belief in themselves to successfully face the opportunities and obstacles that inevitably lie ahead of them.

To teach these skills, she challenged her students with a fascinating assignment. Working in teams, they were tasked with generating as much money as possible with two simple things: $5 in seed money and two hours of time. Students could spend as much time as they wanted in planning. However, when the envelope with $5 was opened, the two-hour timeclock started. They could begin anytime on or after Wednesday afternoon and had to offer a class presentation on Monday afternoon on their success. Students were encouraged to use their entrepreneurial skills in looking for opportunities, questioning assumptions, and creatively utilizing their limited resources.

Seelig reported that the teams garnering the most money ignored the $5, realizing that it put a tight frame around the challenge. They reinterpreted the challenge question into one of how to make the most money with no start-up funds at all. They became acute problem-finders. One team saw the time wasted in standing in line at area restaurants. They made reservations at multiple restaurants and sold them to those customers who gladly avoided the wait. Another team sold air; they charged fellow students to fill their bicycle tires. In fact, their income increased even more when they asked for donations rather than asking for a specified amount. Other teams ran a carwash, sold maps during the school's parent weekend, set up a photo booth during an event, and sold t-shirts to the other students in the class.

The winning team, however, examined the challenge and realized something monumentally important. What could be most potentially valuable was the three minutes of presentation on the ensuing Monday. These students sold their time to a company seeking to recruit students, and the team members developed a commercial for it during their allotted 180 seconds. "This was fabulous," Seelig noted, "They recognized that they had a fabulously valuable asset—that others didn't even notice—just waiting to be mined" (2009, p. 5).

SCAMPER code: Put to other uses. The winning team had the same three minutes of presentation time that the other teams did. They simply used it differently, earning the most money as a result.

Question for creative thought: Questions help to guide the path toward possible solutions. How else can a challenge in your life be reframed through questions?

Sources

Seelig, T. (2009). *What I wish I knew when I was 20: A crash course on making your place in the world.* HarperOne.

Seelig, T. (2015). *Insight out: Get ideas out of your head and into the world.* HarperOne.

Chapter 16

CQ: How Might People Living in Poverty Be Helped?

CPS: Dr. Muhammad Yunus would likely say that, at one point, he knew nothing about banking. After earning his Ph.D. in Economic Development from Vanderbilt University, he returned to his native country of Bangladesh in 1971, the year the country gained independence. After initial excitement, he began "to dread his own lectures" because of his awareness of many in the area suffering financially. From his conversations with people in poverty, he learned that a few dollars could change their lives by freeing them from financial obligations from loan sharks. Dr. Yunus wanted to loan money to villagers—all it would have taken was US $27—but bankers were resistant, believing that the loans would never be repaid. Once Dr. Yunus started to personally guarantee the loans, success followed, and the loan program was extended to other local villages. He repeatedly urged bankers to loan to people directly; they continued to refuse.

Finally, Dr. Yunus organized his own bank in 1983, despite knowing little about the business. His approach was unconventional by Bangladeshi ways. He took his efforts to local villages instead of having a headquarters in the city center. No collateral was required for loans, which were also made to women despite local clerics' desires. Resistance ensued. Some claimed that the bank went against Islam; others claimed that Dr. Yunus and his staff were communists or Christian missionaries.

Through patience and determination, he succeeded to the point where, in six years, half of the borrowers were women. Loans were given to people who begged, allowing them to become entrepreneurs through door-to-door sales or personal sales for those in villages.

In 2011, Dr. Yunus was forced to retire, yet he still maintained, "Human creativity is limitless." Small changes are truly worthwhile, he added, noting that his own journey started from merely loaning $27 to local villagers. Prior to retirement, Dr. Yunus was the recipient of a Nobel Peace Prize in 2006. Called a "banker to the poor," he was honored for his work in helping people escape from poverty and teaching them financial ways to improve their economic status.

SCAMPER code: Modify. Bank loans were still being made, but Dr. Yunus transformed the way they were done.

Question for creative thought: Imagine that Dr. Yunus was on your personal board of advisors in life. What might he suggest to help you work on a creative challenge in your life?

Sources

Les Prix Nobel. (n.d.). *Muhammad Yunus: Biographical*. The Nobel Prize. https://www.nobelprize.org/prizes/peace/2006/yunus/biographical/

Segal, G. Z. (2015). *Getting there: A book of mentors*. Abrams Image. See pp. 135 and 139 for direct quotes.

Chapter 17

CQ: How Can My Time Be of Value to Others?

CPS: Fill in the rest of this question: "Hey, do you know of a good…?" Possible answers are abundant, including plumber, accountant, tutor, physician, hair stylist, physical therapist, and fitness coach. After all, we likely hire more often than we realize. Consider large-scale events and all of the people involved in their success. At a large wedding, a wedding planner, of course, may be a key figure. Additional responsibilities include the officiant, the caterer, the organist, the flower person, and the chauffeur for the limousine.

Jen Glantz's creativity took the idea one step further in answering the question, "Where could I find a good bridesmaid?" A ludicrous question, you might say. After all, people in the wedding party, including bridesmaids, are often relatives or close friends. "Hiring" a bridesmaid would be unthinkable.

Glantz is a professional bridesmaid, an avenue for brides since 2014, and an innovation sparked by what was likely a passing comment. After being asked to be a bridesmaid by two different friends on the same day, her apartment mate suggested that she become a professional. "It was a light bulb moment," she described, leading her to an advertisement—with significant results—on Craigslist. "I knew I was on to something." In 2015, her work took her to over 40 weddings. There was steady growth and she exceeded that number in 2016. Her website gathered over 10,000 applications from people seeking work with her business.

SCAMPER code: Substitute. Her creative niche isn't replacing the need for a bridesmaid. Rather it is substituting who might serve that pivotal role at a wedding.

Question for creative thought: Everyone has a special skill, ability, or personality trait that can help a community. Is there a community volunteer avenue that would cater to your unique skill set?

Source

Snowdon, C. (2016, August 15). *The bridesmaid who comes at a price*. BBC News. https://www.bbc.com/news/business-37052700

Chapter 18

CQ: Paper or Plastic or…?

CPS: When checking out at grocery stores, customers used to be asked, "Paper or plastic?" in reference to the type of bags that they desired. This "paper or plastic" query also has another context: How would you like to pay for something—with cash or with a card? However, the options now extend to electronic with the ability to pay by phone.

Sweden is one country where that question may be becoming obsolete. Cash may be a relic of the past as the country approaches a cash-free system. After all, church tithes have become electronic, and vendors on the street have mobile credit card devices. Many banks don't use cash anymore, removing the temptation for potential bank robbers, and a mere 2% of the country's economy is based on bills or coins. "No one uses cash," said a 23-year-old college student. "I think our generation can live without it." At the same time, she admitted that cashless transactions make it easier to spend without thinking it through.

The trend ripples into other segments of Swedish society. One person selling magazines for a charitable organization has seen a 30% increase in sales since using a mobile card device. Prospective customers with an "I don't have any change" excuse no longer have that out. Another person noted that church congregants donate more in a cashless system because the electronic process is easier. Similar to banks, churches have saved money without devoting money to security costs.

SCAMPER code: Eliminate. The move toward a cash-free economy eliminates the physical exchange of money or goods—an idea which was once unthinkable.

Question for creative thought: The following joke hits the core of elimination. A person believes that someone is living under his bed.

He consults a psychiatrist, who tells him that a cure is possible in three sessions at $300/visit. He tells the psychiatrist that he'll think about it further. The two people meet on the street six months later, and the psychiatrist asks the man why he didn't follow up. There was no need, the man explained, as a bartender cured the problem for $10…by telling him to cut off the legs to the bed. Is there a place where "elimination" creativity could be beneficial in your life?

Sources

Alderman, L. (2015, December 26). In Sweden, a cash-free future nears. *The New York Times*. https://www.nytimes.com/2015/12/27/business/international/in-sweden-a-cash-free-future-nears.html

McRobbie, L. R. (2015, January 8). The ATM is dead. Long live the ATM! *Smithsonian Magazine*. https://www.smithsonianmag.com/history/atm-dead-long-live-atm-180953838/

Miller, M. (2016, October). Laughter: The best medicine. *Reader's Digest*. See pp. 78–79.

Chapter 19

CQ: How Else Can Barbers Uplift a Community?

CPS: It admittedly sounds like the start of a joke. "So, two physicians walk into a bar...bershop." In this case, though, it's not a joke, but a movement where health services connect with patients in a barbershop.

Barbershops aren't just for haircuts—they are much more than that, as viewed by Teo-Carlo Staun, MD. They are a nexus where men can gather, even when no haircut is needed. "There are few other places where men can sit for 30 minutes and just talk. It's almost like therapy," he added (Levin, 2011).

Barbershop screenings for hypertension and diabetes started in California and spread to Worcester, Massachusetts, among other places. The program in Massachusetts, entitled the Mosaic Cultural Complex, was an outgrowth of "Soulful Sundays" that had started in 2002, where men of color would meet informally to talk about difficult pasts with addiction or crime. In 2010, a pilot program of the Barbershop Health Network blossomed as a partnership among the city's social service, government, medical, and private sectors. The Worcester program had one key difference from the California beginnings: It also included mental health screenings for depression and anxiety.

Subsequent initiatives and research support the link between healthcare and barbershops. Victor et al. found a reduction in blood pressure at the 6-month mark among a sample of 319 black male customers from over 50 black-owned barbershops where a pharmacy-generated intervention was conducted. While the control group consisted of men encouraged by their barber to make changes in lifestyle or to talk to physicians, the intervention group centered on the barbers doing the screening and subsequently referring participants to pharmacists located in the barbershop. A pediatrician writing about the study in *The New York Times* observed, "Getting barbers involved meant health messages came from trusted members of the community," which is also perhaps the reason for the high rate of participants in the study remaining in it throughout its entirety.

Meanwhile, in Indianapolis, as an outgrowth of "The Confess Project," Lorenzo Lewis is also training barbers on warning signs of depression and anxiety. Lorenzo believes that barbers can become effective mental health advocates for black men.

SCAMPER code: Modification. These everyday innovators have taken something—in this case, barbershops—and added value to it. Rather than solely focusing on hair, barbers can also help their patrons become healthier.

Question for creative thought: How can your roles in life be modified (even slightly) to add more value to your personal or professional world?

Sources

Carroll, A. E. (2018, May 18). What barbershops can teach about delivering health care. *The New York Times.* https://www.nytimes.com/2018/05/21/upshot/what-barbershops-can-teach-about-delivering-health-care.html

Levin, A. (2011, July 15). *Some barbershops aren't just for haircuts anymore.* Psychiatric News. https://psychnews.psychiatryonline.org/doi/full/10.1176/pn.46.14.psychnews_46_14_9

Mullins, M. (2019, September 10). *Organization trains barbers to be mental health advocates.* RTV6 Indianapolis. https://www.theindychannel.com/lifestyle/health/organization-trains-barbers-to-be-mental-health-advocates

Victor, R. G., Lynch, K., Li, N., Blyler, C., Muhammad, E., Handler, J., Brettler, J., Rashid, M., Hsu, B., Foxx-Drew, D., Moy, N., Reid, A. E., & Elashoff, R. M. (2018). A cluster-randomized trial of blood-pressure reduction in black barbershops. *New England Journal of Medicine, 378*(14), 1291–1301.

Chapter 20

CQ: How Can More Customers Be Drawn to a Restaurant?

CPS: Happy hour is traditionally connected with late afternoon discounts on alcohol as a way for restaurateurs to entice pre-dinner customers. However, happy hours didn't originally revolve around alcohol. According to Peter Jensen Brown, the origin of happy hour extends as far back as 1914 when the United States Navy organized weekly entertainment to help sailors with boredom while at sea. When Prohibition arrived in 1920, people would meet at speakeasies or at friends' homes to drink prior to dinner, and the term *happy hour* began to refer instead to this clandestine get-together.

Instead of pre-dinner time for happy hour, some establishments have creatively employed it at the "opposite" time. One restaurant in Pittsburgh, Pennsylvania, split happy hour in two: 4:30–5:30 p.m. and 7:30–8:30 p.m. Another place engineered a 9–11 p.m. happy hour on weekend nights. One manager noted that customers appreciate the later times and how they have added business, particularly on Sunday evenings. Another manager pointed to the Sunday evening happy hour times being sensitive to those who can't make it during afternoon times, including those who are chefs, bartenders, and servers.

SCAMPER code: Rearrange. Switching up a time commonly set for something like happy hour is one way to redefine it and reach customers in a new way.

Question for creative thought: Conner and Silvia found that positive affect, such as excitement and enthusiasm, was a strong predictor of daily creativity. With this in mind, what activities bring you happiness and how might they contribute to your creative thinking?

Sources

Conner, T. S., & Silvia, P. J. (2015). Creative days: A daily diary study of emotion, personality, and everyday creativity. *Psychology of Aesthetics, Creativity, and the Arts*, *9*(4), 463–470. https://doi.org/10.1037/aca0000022.supp

Harrop, J. K. (2020, January 24). *Cheers! Some bars and restaurants offer late-night happy hours*. TribLive. https://triblive.com/lifestyles/more-lifestyles/cheers-some-bars-and-restaurants-offer-late-night-happy-hours/

Herreria, C. (2016, April 6). *So THAT'S why it's called happy hour*. HuffPost. https://www.huffpost.com/entry/history-of-happy-hour_n_56fc8afee4b0daf53aeeb6fa

Chapter 21

CQ: How Can I Send a Letter Without Knowing the Address?

CPS: Despite the advent of email and other forms of electronic communication, snail mail lives. The United States Postal Service handles over 187 million first-class items each day. Over 5,600 pieces of mail are processed each *second*. Over 75,000 carriers make the drive to neighborhoods throughout the United States and deliver mail by walking from address to address. In certain areas of Florida and Arizona, creativity is seen firsthand: Carriers make deliveries by bicycle.

Children learn that the process of mailing a letter starts with addressing the envelope. After all, the recipient's name, the house number and street name, and the town, state or province, and postal code are important. Right? Perhaps not, at least in one case.

In 2016, a woman in western Iceland was surprised to receive a letter. It had no address. Rather, a map, a description, and a clue were on the envelope, all of which were sufficient enough for the Icelandic mail carrier to find the horse farm where the recipient lived. In lieu of an address, the sender offered a map of the believed location of the farm along with the following: "Country: Iceland. City: Búðardalur. Name: A horse farm with an Icelandic/Danish couple and three kids and a lot of sheep!" To give the postal system even more help, the sender added a clue about where the recipient worked ("a supermarket in Búðardalur").

The sender of the letter, a tourist who had stayed at the horse farm, demonstrated one creative principle discussed in the Introduction: Question assumptions. According to creativity coach Jurgen Wolff, all challenges have assumptions, to the point that they "seem so obvious that most people never think to challenge them." Kudos to the tourist for not assuming that all letters needed a proper address.

SCAMPER code: Adapt. Dealing with the information at hand, the letter-sender adjusted the address—with success.

Question for creative thought: Take a peek at your business card. (If you do not have a business card, then feel free to imagine one in your mind.) How you are "addressed"? In what way does your business card describe your role, and in what creative way might you alter your title? A 2017 BBC article discussed the inflation in job titles, as more senior titles were given to more employees. In the article, Brown noted, "Since a powerful-sounding job title can signify social status, it's not surprising workers aspire to them, often without the salary or responsibilities to match."

Sources

BBC Trending. (2016, August 31). *Letter gets there by hand-drawn map*. https://www.bbc.com/news/blogs-trending-37233913

Brown, J. (2017, September 20). *Can a job title change your behavior?* BBC Worklife. https://www.bbc.com/worklife/article/20170920-can-a-job-title-can-change-your-behaviour

United States Postal Service. (n.d.). *One day in the life of the U.S. Postal Service*. https://facts.usps.com/one-day/

Wolff, J. (2012). *Creativity now*. Pearson. See p. 78.

Chapter 22

CQ: Where Can I Look for New Ideas?

CPS: Creativity expert Michael Michalko wrote, "The most creative force is nature," and innovations based on Mother Nature are numerous. Wolff cited multiple examples, including the inspiration of new plastics from sea cucumbers' ability to thicken its skin and the redesign of swimsuits from the study of shark skin. The same skin helped engineers at Airbus create a new foil to coat its planes' wings. Ever wear snowshoes? Biologist and biomimicry expert Janine Benyus offered the example of individuals of Native American ancestry who watched the snowshoe hare navigating snow with its large hind feet. They went on to build snowshoes in the same way, allowing them to float above the snow. A gecko's toe pad can stick and unstick to surfaces, and a mature gecko can support over 290 pounds. Both of these features prompted leaders at Ford to wonder if they could design adhesives with similar properties for use in their cars.

With creativity, the Pike Syndrome may apply. Linkner described an experiment where a pike, a fish known for fierceness, was placed in a tank with smaller fish. However, the pike was separated from the fish by a glass layer. Repeatedly the pike unsuccessfully attacked the fish, only to collide with the glass. Eventually the pike gave up, sinking to the bottom of the tank, at which point the scientists removed the glass barrier. The pike could then swim freely, eating the smaller fish with ease, yet it didn't. The other fish were ignored; the pike died of starvation. Pike Syndrome, then, is a paralysis by imaginary barriers, a condition that calls for adapting to the changing environment.

SCAMPER code: Put to other uses. Putting an idea to use in a different context is the essence of biomimicry. If you're seeking creative inspiration, a visit to nature may help. As executive Tim Brown said, "Borrowing from the outside world is at the heart of all things we do creatively to be inspired."

Question for creative thought: Visit a zoo, either real or imaginary, or a wildlife sanctuary. Observe how animals have special abilities. How might one of their unique abilities help you with a stressful situation that you currently face?

Sources

AAA Motorist. (2016, February). *Carmakers seek solutions by mimicking nature*. See p. 22.

Linkner, J. (2011). *Disciplined dreaming: A proven system to drive breakthrough creativity*. Jossey-Bass.

Michalko, M. (2011). *Creative thinkering*. New World Library. See p. 53.

Walters, H. (2014, February 7). *The world's best creative director: Nature*. Ideas.TED.com. https://ideas.ted.com/nature-knows-best-a-biologist-and-a-designer-take-creative-direction-from-the-earths-operating-system/

Wolff, J. (2012). *Creativity now*. Pearson.

Chapter 23

CQ: How Might the Olympics Inspire Other Populations?

CPS: Spectators and fans across the globe follow the Olympics, both Summer and Winter, as well as the Paralympic Games and the Special Olympics. The 2016 Summer Olympics in Brazil attracted 3.6 billion viewers. Doubtlessly, a fraction of these viewers were elderly residents in Switzerland. However, their Olympic participation went even further when the association that coordinates the retirement homes in the region held its own Olympic games for residents. Instead of a 100-meter sprint or a beach volleyball match, these Olympians had other events, such as pounding nails into blocks of wood. One 90-year-old participant was quoted as appreciating the incentive of the event: "It pushes us a little, it's always quiet in our rooms and then all of a sudden this happens… it's a good initiative," she said.

In these Swiss Olympic games, 120 elderly competitors participated, with the oldest at age 96. Similar to the real Olympics, winning medals was a part of the festivities; the medals were awarded by Eri Hanni, a native to the area in Switzerland and a silver medalist in judo at the 1964 Tokyo Games.

SCAMPER code: Modify. In addition to nationality, Olympic athletes can range in age and ability. The types of competition also change.

Question for creative thought: A 2018 article on the Team USA website outlined changes to events planned for the Olympic Summer Games in Tokyo. For instance, the Games feature new events in the arenas of canoe/kayak and cycling. If you were a member of the committee organizing Olympic events, what completely new and fun-to-watch competition would you propose?

Sources

News from Elsewhere. (2016, September 14). *Swiss seniors compete in 'elderly Olympics.'* BBC News. https://www.bbc.com/news/blogs-news-from-elsewhere-37351192

Kortemeier, T. (2018, July 24). *A complete look at all the new sports and events for the Olympic Games Tokyo 2020*. Team USA. https://www.teamusa.org/News/2018/July/24/A-Complete-Look-At-All-The-New-Sports-And-Events-For-The-Olympic-Games-Tokyo-2020

Statista. (2019, March 4). *Number of Olympic Games TV viewers worldwide from 2002 to 2016*. https://www.statista.com/statistics/287966/olympic-games-tv-viewership-worldwide/

Chapter 24

CQ: Is There a Word for That?

CPS: People can communicate in all kinds of different ways, and language is just one of them—an efficient means to boot. We use words with little consideration of their origin. We don't have to stop and analyze the meaning of each word before speaking it. After all, language is a creative way to communicate.

Words are "invented" each year. Merriam-Webster added 533 new words to its dictionary in 2019. A *solopreneur* may have taken a *vacay* that had *fabulosity*, meaning that an entrepreneur working by themselves took a vacation with fabulous qualities. The question, of course, is whether they played *pickleball* or tried an *escape room*—other new words—during that getaway.

Yet the creativity instilled in a language may not be all-encompassing. In other words, words for certain concepts, feelings, or situations may be missing. For example, *zeg* in Georgian means the "day after tomorrow." The sense that you will fall in love with another person upon meeting them refers to *koi no yokan* in Japanese. Moving hot food around in your mouth until you can eat it is *pelini* in the Buli language in Ghana. These examples show that there is plenty more room for new words in English.

In language, the notion of conceptual blending—the creation of various patterns in thinking—comes into play with words. Verbally blending different combinations of words makes new meanings, such as *finger lakes*, *conference call*, and *race card* (Michalko, 2011). Combining concepts in different ways alters meaning. More unique combinations equate to more unique meanings. As Michalko wrote, "The blend then bubbles up in the form of ideas and insights. This transcends logical thinking. This is creative thinking."

SCAMPER code: Adapt. Language is constantly being adapted. Listen to a toddler learn to speak, and chances are that you will hear numerous (and creative) adaptations.

Question for creative thought: When my children were younger, I invited all of us to make up new words. (Mine was *chatelachmine*…I thought it sounded like some kind of new food additive.) Take a moment with a friend and invent a funny-sounding word. Now add four or six or even ten to the list. What did you come up with? Have fun making up entertaining definitions that inevitably make you both laugh. Periodically, when together, use the fictitious word like a real word when one (or both) of you needs a chuckle.

Sources

Merriam-Webster. (2019, September 17). *We added new words to the dictionary for September 2019.* https://www.merriam-webster.com/words-at-play/new-words-in-the-dictionary

Michalko, M. (2011). *Creative thinkering.* New World Library. See p. 23.

The Week Staff. (2013, January 15). *14 wonderful words with no English equivalent.* https://theweek.com/articles/468753/14-wonderful-words-no-english-equivalent

Chapter 25

CQ: How Can Food Mix with Social Change?

CPS: People choose restaurants for all kinds of reasons: the cost, the ambience, the location, the service, and, of course, the quality of the food. Restaurants often have themes or features, such as an indoor playground, magicians that go from table to table, or certain artwork featured on the walls.

One pop-up café in Indonesia has a rather unusual theme. Customers visiting the Jamban Café sit on toilets. Serving bowls are replaced by toilet bowls. "You would think it's gross and unhygienic," said one customer. "It's not something you expect." Another customer commented that he didn't try any food until his third visit. However, the meals are free at the Jamban Café, and a specific goal is behind the toilet-based theme: The hope is that this arrangement adds pressure on the government to offer improved sanitation in a country where at least 50 million people lack access to a clean toilet. The owner related that the idea behind the café is to heighten awareness and initiate a dialogue about sanitation needs.

SCAMPER code: Combine. Mingling two items that wouldn't ordinarily be put together—toilets and restaurants—is a creative attempt to point attention toward sanitation needs.

Questions for creative thought: The concept of gator brain fits with the Jamban Café model. According to Hurson, an alligator may do one of a few things if it sees something new and strange in the swamp: fight it, flee from it, eat it, simply freeze, or try to mate with it. What were your initial reactions with the Jamban Café? Did you fight, freeze, or flee from this different idea for an eatery, or are you willing to engage with the idea?

Sources

BBC News. (2016, August 16). *Indonesian toilet café aims to educate and entertain*. https://www.bbc.com/news/av/world-asia-37081711/indonesian-toilet-cafe-aims-to-educate-and-entertain

Hurson, T. (2008). *Think better*. McGraw-Hill. See page 21.

Chapter 26

CQ: Can a Hotel Be Put on Wheels?

CPS: People sleep on trains, on planes, and in cars, though perhaps not comfortably. They sleep on cruise ships and may nod off during a ferry commute. In some places they can also get a good night's sleep on buses; two California entrepreneurs have developed a way for a hotel-like atmosphere on a bus. Their bus line, called Cabin, features a WiFi-equipped lounge with leather seats as well as sleeping pods with privacy curtains and pressed sheets.

The idea, in the words of one of the entrepreneurs, is to turn trips "into an experience where you're basically checking into a hotel in one city and then checking out of a hotel in another city." The buses travel overnight, making jaunts between Los Angeles to San Francisco while providing an atmosphere where comfortable sleep is possible. Drivers use apps to collect data on changes in bus speed and vibration, which is used to find the smoothest route possible for customer rest. The hope is to make the bus suspension smooth enough so that passengers aren't able to detect whether they are even on a road. Piloted as "Sleep Bus" in 2016, the overnight bus-in-comfort idea found instant success, selling out of tickets in the first three days.

SCAMPER code: Combine. Bringing hotel-like features to a bus is one way to make it unique.

Question for creative thought: If vehicles can be used to sell ice cream, lunches (think food truck), and now sleep, how else could they be used in innovative ways?

Source

Holley, P. (2017, August 10). Can a better night's sleep in a 'hipster' bus replace flying? *The Washington Post*. https://www.washingtonpost.com/news/innovations/wp/2017/08/10/can-a-better-nights-sleep-in-a-hipster-bus-replace-flying/

Chapter 27

CQ: What Else Can a Library Offer?

CPS: Travel to any remote corner of the county or state and you'll likely find a public library in the vicinity. Nearly 17,000 public libraries are scattered throughout the United States, a number that surpasses the number of McDonald's restaurants. According to one estimate, Americans visit a library—school, public, or academic—three times more often than going to a movie theater. In 2015, all told, librarians saw 1.39 billion visits to public libraries.

The draw of a public library is more than the books. As the director of the Institute of Museum and Library Services said, libraries are expanding in scope: "Libraries are offering more programs on everything from early childhood to workforce resources, and public participation is also rising."

Yet, sometimes there is more. A visit to Anchorage, Alaska, will uncover a unique library where more than books can be checked out. Patrons at a library on the University of Alaska campus can choose animals to take home. Need a carcass of a ring-necked pheasant? The library has it. The same goes for a mounted black rockfish. The library boasts hundreds of similar items, all of which are available with an Anchorage library card. The snowy owl is a popular item for Harry Potter parties. You may not be surprised to know that this library is the only one of its kind in the United States.

SCAMPER code: Put to other uses. The Alaska Resources Library and Information Services capitalizes on how a library can offer options besides literature.

Question for creative thought: Create a new type of library similar to the one described above. What would it loan, and how could it aid patrons?

Sources

American Library Association. (2012). Quotable facts about America's libraries. http://www.ala.org/aboutala/sites/ala.org.aboutala/files/content/QuotableFacts.2012_0.pdf

Institute of Museum and Library Services. (2018, August 2). *People visited public libraries more than a billion times in 2015*. https://www.imls.gov/news/people-visited-public-libraries-more-billion-times-2015

Nalewicki, J. (2019, April 18). This library in Anchorage lends out taxidermic specimens. *Smithsonian Magazine*. https://www.smithsonianmag.com/travel/library-anchorage-lends-out-taxidermy-specimens-180971948/

Chapter 28

CQ: Can Rivers, Lakes, and Oceans Be Made Cleaner?

CPS: Boyan Slat could be described as a good problem-finder. He has been an inventor and builder since childhood, yet, in looking back, said, "I liked problem-solving, but what I didn't really have was a real problem to work on." Slat finally found a big problem when scuba diving in Greece, where he saw more plastic bags than fish during his dives. Despite others' skepticism that the garbage could be collected, he returned to the Netherlands and created a foundation, The Ocean Cleanup, in 2013.

His idea of a cleaning system came to him when he was 16 and worked on a flipped concept. Instead of going after patches of water garbage, how about if the garbage moved to the cleaning devices via ocean currents? To further dedicate his attention to solving the dilemma, Slat disenrolled from his aerospace engineering program, and, in the same year, delivered a TEDx talk that went viral with a subsequent interest level of 1,500 emails per day. Working with engineers and other experts, Slat completed a prototype in 2016, putting it to work in the North Sea. His optimism in future technologies is clear, as he said, "As long as we develop technologies that actually help solve problems, I think eventually we will get to a pretty bright future."

The Ocean Cleanup has a goal of reducing plastic floating on the ocean surface by 90% by 2040. A solar-powered device to prevent plastic from entering oceans from rivers has already been created.

SCAMPER code: Reverse. Reversing the process is what Slat's idea is all about. Instead of finding waste, allow the waste to find the cleaning device.

Question for creative thought: Slat's invention makes me think of a filter or a screen, the concept of which is helpful in this situation. In the case of creative thinking, however, filters created by the brain may be a deterrent because they can inhibit some good ideas from finding their way to the conscious mind. As Mlodinow wrote, "Our brains may make unusual and useful associations, only to have them discarded." How might your cognitive screen be holding back creative ideas, and how might the screen allow more of those creative gems through?

Sources

Gaines, J. (2016, July 7). *This young inventor's brilliant device could remove tons of garbage from our oceans.* Upworthy. https://www.upworthy.com/this-young-inventors-brilliant-device-could-remove-tons-of-garbage-from-our-oceans

Mlodinow, L. (2018). *Elastic: Flexible thinking in a time of change*. Pantheon Books. See p. 174.

The Ocean Cleanup. (n.d.). *We are The Ocean Cleanup.* https://theoceancleanup.com/about/

Chapter 29

CQ: Are There Other Ways to Land Airplanes?

CPS: Hurson differentiated two types of thinking: reproductive and productive. The former is doing what you did in the past and thinking the way that you previously thought. "Mindless repetition" would be one way to describe the extreme end of reproductive thinking if it were on a continuum. It is of value when the high consequences of failure exist. Hurson offered the example of a pilot landing a plane. "You don't want your airline pilot, coming in for a landing, to muse, 'Hmm, I wonder what would happen if I tried it this way.'" Rather the passengers want pilots to rely on what they always did in the frequently repeated landing.

But what if there were a different, perhaps better, way to land the plane? One Dutch engineer thinks that there is and has spent years researching this idea. Working out of the Netherlands Aerospace Centre, Henk Hesselink proposed the idea of circular runways. His inspiration struck while watching treacherous airliner landings on YouTube, and, through the use of simulation, he has tested the idea of circular runways. In his modeling, as many as three planes could depart and land at the same time. Hesselink maintained that, by virtue of a runway redesign, airports would be less noisy, more climate-friendly, and more efficient in regard to airplane traffic. Another idea by Hesselink is to build offices and parking garages under the runways to help heat runways in icy conditions.

SCAMPER code: Rearrange. Changing the shape of traditional runways can also solve some of the airports' other issues.

Question for creative thought: "Going in circles" is a phrase associated with being unproductive. One aviation example is when airplanes circle airports during times of high air traffic. However, apply the circular runway idea to your life. Are there times when going in circles can help you solve problems you encounter?

Sources

Hurson, T. (2008). *Think better*. McGraw-Hill. See especially pages 38 and 47.

Shaw, D. (2017, March 16). *Think again: Will circular runways ever take off?* BBC News. https://www.bbc.com/news/av/magazine-39284294/think-again-will-circular-runways-ever-take-off

Shaw, D. (2017, April 21). *Circular runways: Engineer defends his proposal*. BBC News. https://www.bbc.com/news/magazine-39643292

Chapter 30

CQ: How Can Older Adults Be More Active?

CPS: Consider common stereotypes of older adults: They are seen as sedentary, less healthy, and in cognitive decline. However, those misconceptions are not necessarily representative when we look at three rather creative ways that older adults are keeping in shape, both physically and mentally, in different countries.

In Cosmo City, South Africa, older women have taken to boxing, not only as a way to keep fit, but also as a form of self-defense. The program enrolls those 60 years of age and older, with one 75-year-old member saying, "I like boxing. Whenever I train, I feel younger, I don't feel pains." The coach, at age 40, said that he discovered that the women were not as fragile as he anticipated, adding that in essence he was actually the student: "They ended up training me," he said, "instead of me training them because their energy level was just too high."

Two creative activities for older citizens arise in South Korea. Teams of women ages 70 and older engage in a modification of aerobics, called "cheerobics." These cheerobics squads appear in shows and competitions. A member of one team with an average age of 74 compared cheerobics to a husband: It was always with her, adding comfort and happiness to her life. Another team member credited cheerobics with helping her overcome depression, while another woman pointed to her increased aerobic capacity in her six years on the team. The team's cohesiveness is quite evident: One person commented that she is closer to those on the team than to her actual siblings.

The local government in Seoul brought an activity associated with nighttime into daytime. Disco dancing, complete with the disco ball and lights, is offered to older adults as a way to combat loneliness and dementia. The over-65 events have been a success; one man noticed that, after a few visits to the disco, some people were tossing aside their canes. "This club is like medicine to me!" one woman exclaimed. Despite having a bad back and legs, one person noticed that his pain disappears when the music starts, giving him additional energy in the subsequent two or three days as well. Other benefits include the social activity; one person smiled as he said that he found a girlfriend through his visits to the club. "There's no place like this in the world," another man said. "I hope this spreads around the world so every older person can be happy and healed."

SCAMPER codes: Put to other uses, Substitute, Rearrange. With these three examples, we can apply several different SCAMPER codes. For example, boxing in South Africa is being put to a different use, cheerobics is a substitute for traditional aerobics, and Seoul's senior disco rearranges the traditional dance time from nighttime to daytime.

Questions for creative thought: A common stereotype of older individuals evolves around limited mobility and overall activity. Prior to reading this story, how would you have responded to the idea of grandmothers who box or a cheer team of older women? How might stereotypes limit your creativity?

Sources

Lang, O., & Lee, J. Y. (producers). (2019, August 27). *Seoul's over-65s disco 'like medicine' for seniors* [video]. BBC News. https://www.bbc.com/news/av/world-asia-49448760/seoul-s-over-65s-disco-like-medicine-for-seniors

Lang, O., Lee, J. Y., & Do, Y. (2019, September 9). *'Age is just a number' for senior cheerobics team* [video]. BBC News. https://www.bbc.com/news/av/world-asia-49595000/age-is-just-a-number-for-senior-cheerobics-team

Parkinson, C. (2017, August 28). *South Africa's boxing grannies*. BBC News. https://www.bbc.com/news/av/world-africa-41055076

Chapter 31

CQ: Are Coffee Grounds Really Just Waste?

CPS: A 2017 survey found that nearly half (44%) of Americans drank 2–3 cups of coffee each day. (Shockingly, 2% drank 11 or more cups daily!) Coffee consumption seems to be stable in recent years, though the average fell to 1.6 cups per day in 2016. Age is a correlate of use as well: Those who are 18–19 years of age average about a cup per day, while those who are 70 and older drink about three times as much. In 2011, the United States led the world in coffee consumption, drinking 400 million cups each day. In fact, 55% of coffee users reported that they would rather gain 10 pounds than abstain from the beverage for the rest of their lives.

All in all, coffee is omnipresent in the United States. It is evident that the supply of coffee waste will be ever-ready in the United Kingdom as well; about 500,000 tons of coffee is consumed annually there. With so much coffee, though, what happens to the grounds that remain after a fresh pot is brewed? British entrepreneur Arthur Kay has an answer: Use the waste for fuel to power vehicles. Kay's idea hatched in 2013, and he went on to become the founder and deputy chairman of bio-bean, the first factory in the world to recycle coffee. Oil can be extracted from coffee grounds and converted into pellets for wood burners. His company has also worked on using coffee grounds to fuel city buses. In 2019, bio-bean partnered with Stansted Airport, helping it to become the first airport in the world to convert its coffee waste into biofuels. Over six million cups are consumed at the airport annually, translating into 150 tons of subsequent waste.

Kay's work has decreased greenhouse gas emissions from landfills, particularly when considering that coffee grains give off methane, a greenhouse gas that is at least 28 times more potent than carbon dioxide. The United Nations labeled his company as "a climate action innovator."

SCAMPER code: Put to other uses. Taking beverage remains and using them for fuel is an innovative way to decrease waste and power vehicles.

Question for creative thought: Seelig related a delightful story about asking students to find items of value in a trash can and put them together to create something of even more value. Look at the sundry items in the wastebasket closest to you. How could they be combined to become valuable to others?

Sources

Kunst, A. (2019, December 19). *U.S. consumer: daily coffee drinking consumption 2017*. Statista. https://www.statista.com/statistics/250230/americans-daily-coffee-consumption/

Kitchen Daily. (2011, November 2). *America's coffee obsession: Fun facts that prove we're hooked*. HuffPost. https://www.huffpost.com/entry/americas-coffee-obsession_n_987885

London Stansted Airport Mag. (2019, October 17). *London Stansted to become first airport in the world to convert all its coffee waste to solid biofuels in ground-breaking partnership with bio-bean*. https://mediacentre.stanstedairport.com/london-stansted-to-become-first-airport-in-world-to-convert-all-its-coffee-waste-to-solid-biofuels-in-ground-breaking-partnership-with-bio-bean/

Seelig, T. (2012). *inGenius: A crash course on creativity*. HarperOne.

United Nations Global Compact. (2017). *Arthur Kay*. https://www.unglobalcompact.org/sdgs/sdgpioneers/2017/arthur-kay

Wakefield, J. (2017, June 15). *Future energy: Will buses be run on coffee?* BBC News. https://www.bbc.com/news/technology-38854886

Chapter 32

CQ: Is Vision Necessary to Play Baseball?

CPS: Historians may know the name "Charlie Fairbanks," vice president of the United States from 1905 to 1909. However, when it comes to creativity, another Charlie Fairbanks arises. This Mr. Fairbanks found a problem in the question above: Can people with vision difficulties play baseball? As an engineer working for a telephone company, he placed a beeping implant into a softball in 1964 to help people with visual impairment play baseball. About a decade later, the National Beep Baseball Association (NBBA) was formed. Games feature a 16-inch ball with a pin that, when pulled, emanates a beeping sound. With the exception of the pitchers and catchers, all players, regardless of visual abilities, are blindfolded. Pitchers throw from 20 feet in front of home plate, utilizing verbal cues to help the batters, their teammates, know when to swing the bat. Four strikes are permitted, and two bases (goals) are used. Spotters, who are sighted helpers in the field, aid players via verbal cues.

Blake Boudreaux, a player who served as the NBBA president in 2017, became visually impaired due to cancer at the age of 5. Referring to the players, he commented, "A lot of these men and women lost their sight later on in life and had played sports prior to, so it was their way to find that competitive outlet again." One player for the Boston Renegades spoke about how the game changed his perspective, saying, "When I play Beep Baseball, I feel like I'm leaving my cane on the bench."

SCAMPER code: Modify. Modifying a baseball revolutionized the game for those with visual impairments.

Question for creative thought: "Ultimately, we see whatever our brains think we should"—this was stated in the opening of a 1993 article on vision and the brain. Neurons dedicated to vision amount to about 30% of neurons, compared to 8% for touch and only 3% for hearing. If your vision was impaired, you'd rely much more on your touch and hearing neurons. Focus on everyday sounds in your life. What sound do you hear often and how might it be applied differently/creatively?

Sources

Grady, D. (1993, June 1). The vision thing: Mainly in the brain. *Discover Magazine.* https://www.discovermagazine.com/mind/the-vision-thing-mainly-in-the-brain. See paragraph 12 for quote.

Light, A. (2017, October 4). *'Beep baseball' brings adapted game to those who are blind, visually impaired.* WBUR: Here and Now. https://www.wbur.org/hereandnow/2017/10/04/beep-baseball?utm_source=iosnewsapp&utm_medium=Email&utm_campaign=app

Markusen, B. (2015, August 4). *Beep baseball a hit in Cooperstown.* National Baseball Hall of Fame. https://baseballhall.org/news/beep-baseball-a-hit-in-cooperstown

Chapter 33

CQ: How Can I Find My Car in a City of Three Million People?

CPS: Michalko outlined important qualities of creativity in writing, "One of the hallmarks of a creative thinker is the ability to tolerate ambiguity, dissonance, inconsistency, and things out of place." In this case study, those last three words—out of place—may be most relevant. In a *Seinfeld* episode, the four characters were meandering through a New Jersey mall parking garage, having "lost" their car. After Kramer seems to recall that the parking space was near an elevator, an exasperated George complained, "There's elevators all over! Everything looks the same. We're like rats in some experiment!"

Garvin Strickland, a 19-year-old from Syracuse, New York, could probably empathize. He drove five hours to Toronto for a Metallica concert but afterward couldn't find his car. Rather, he couldn't remember where he parked the car. He searched all night, but even with Toronto police assisting him, Garvin couldn't recall precisely where he had parked the 2016 Nissan Versa Sedan. On Monday morning, he gave up, taking a bus back to Syracuse.

Then his father had an idea. Would a Craigslist post help?

With a $100 reward attached, the post included all of the information that his son remembered. The car was near a Starbucks and maybe a bank and adjacent to some construction and within a US $8 cab fare from the Rogers Centre, the venue of the concert. Though the leads were minimal, one couple dove into the challenge. "We were a little bored and deciding to go to bed or go on a little adventure in our city," said Madison Riddolls after she and her boyfriend located the Versa. "I felt like I owed it to the family."

Strickland returned to Canada, claimed the car from a parking garage, and returned to Syracuse. The garage even gave Garvin a Bluetooth device to eliminate the possibility of losing the car again.

SCAMPER code: Adapt. We have all seen calls for help in locating lost pets posted throughout a neighborhood. The father's creativity of using Craigslist in a city 250 miles away was one way to blanket the area with "lost car" notices. (Side note: In case you didn't see the *Seinfeld* episode, Jerry and his friends finally found their car.)

Question for creative thought: Sure, you may lose—er, misplace—things often. Cell phone? Eyeglasses? Car keys? Often these items are found, but not without a certain frustration after looking under the sofa cushions 14 times. Years ago a person gave me invaluable advice: If you want to find a lost item, stop looking for it. Inevitably it will resurface. What are creative ways to find things in your life?

Sources

BBC News. (2017, July 21). *Toronto helps 'doofy son' find his parked car four days on*. https://www.bbc.com/news/world-us-canada-40677727

Michalko, M. (2011). *Creative thinkering*. New World Library. See p. 5.

Chapter 34

CQ: How Can a Better Vacuum Cleaner Be Made?

CPS: You have probably seen and maybe even used one of his company's over 60 products. Dissatisfied with his family's vacuum cleaner as a child, he was determined to create a better one. He was successful, and this self-made billionaire developed the world's first vacuum cleaner without a bag. Despite this success, this man does not have an engineering degree. Rather, he attended a London art school.

His name is James Dyson, and he was formally knighted in 2006. He's an inventor who is clearly Pro-C in achievement. Nearly 6,000 engineers work for his global company, which also devotes about $10 million per week to product development. He assisted in the development of a new engineering department at Imperial College London in 2015.

Among Dyson's legacy and achievements is the way he helped take others' innovations to new levels. Around 2004, the James Dyson Foundation launched an annual award for engineering students and recent graduates throughout 27 countries and 100 universities with one goal in mind: designing something to address a real-world challenge. Winners from past years have developed products to address an array of problems, including pollution, conservation, and medical approaches in poorer countries.

The 2019 recipient for the U.K. section was Lucy Hughes, an innovator who came up with an alternative to single-use plastics. Her bioplastic is biodegradable and originates from red algae and products from fishing industry waste. Hughes, a graduate of the University of Sussex, told BBC News about another benefit: "Because it's using a waste material rather than a virgin material, you get that material at a much lower cost or sometimes, you know, free," she said.

Incidentally, for those of you who are parents, a prize for innovation was awarded to clothes that expand as children aged 6 months to 3 years grow. This idea could save both time and money for parents of toddlers.

SCAMPER code: Put to other uses. Sir James Dyson's success in designing a vacuum cleaner has inspired other design accomplishments through academics and his foundation awards.

Question for creative thought: Review the list of projects selected to be finalists for the current competition. If you were in the shoes of Sir James Dyson, which project would be named as the winning idea and why? (This website will tell you more: https://www.jamesdysonaward.org/news/james-dyson-award-top-twenty-announcement/)

Sources

BBC News. (2017, September 9). *Clothes that grow with your child win Dyson prize* [video]. https://www.youtube.com/watch?v=iR87n10u16U

Forbes. (n.d.) *#303 James Dyson.* https://www.forbes.com/profile/james-dyson/#1551f3202b38

The James Dyson Foundation. (n.d.). *The James Dyson Award 2019 opens for entries.* https://www.jamesdysonfoundation.com/news/JDA2019-open-for-entries.html

Lewington, L. (2019, September 19). *Fish waste-based alternative plastic wins Dyson Award.* BBC News. https://www.bbc.com/news/av/technology-49756240/fish-waste-based-alternative-to-plastic-wins-dyson-award

Powley, T. (2015, March 22). Dyson helps launch design engineering school at Imperial College. *Financial Times.* https://www.ft.com/content/73b0b9ac-cf15-11e4-893d-00144feab7de

Rozenberg, G., & Butler, S. (2006, December 30). Dyson, former Lord Mayor and head of Sainsbury's lead business honours. *Times, The (United Kingdom)*, p. 41.

Chapter 35

CQ: How Can I, an Experienced Golfer, Keep Improving My Golf Skills?

CPS: Luck. Dumb luck. Accident. Coincidence. Serendipity—however it is labeled, the question about how this concept collides with creativity is alluring. Alex Osborn, a pioneer in creativity, reasoned that some element of luck may be involved in creative ideas, but the true foundation is inspiration. He wrote, "In the main, luck is the by-product of effort. It is indeed a rare accident when inspiration comes without perspiration."

Professor Richard Wiseman in the United Kingdom has dedicated more than a superficial examination of the topic of luck. In one study, he asked both lucky and unlucky participants (determined based on their scores on various assessments) and found that those who were lucky were higher in life satisfaction and on extraversion, smiling twice as often as those who were unlucky.

The next part of Wiseman's research relates to creativity more closely. It seems that lucky people were more open to experience, which is a strong predictor of creativity. Wiseman noted that those individuals were more likely to travel more often and be receptive to unique possibilities in life. Kaufman, a foremost scholar in creativity, pointed to "openness to experience" as *the* primary item in developing creativity. According to him, this quality translates into curiosity, challenging yourself to move outside your personal area of comfort, and a gratitude for beauty. Other research supports the connection between creativity and openness to experience, showing that the latter trait could also invigorate innovation in organizations.

That openness to life experience can be directed as well—it doesn't require serendipity. Butch Harmon, the top golf instructor in the world for 19 straight years, had been observing another instructor from afar and liked what he saw. Harmon decided to meet the other instructor, who was nearly 30 years younger, and take a lesson from him. "I like people who are different," he said in a *Golf Digest* interview. "I always want to learn from whoever's doing new things." Besides which, the younger instructor was bringing results, and that, Harmon noted, is "what makes a teacher great."

SCAMPER code: Reverse. Instead of looking to an even more experienced instructor for learning, Butch Harmon chose a younger instructor.

Questions for creative thought: Identify an area in which you have an information base you would like to expand. Who could give you a lesson on the topic? What are two questions that you would want answered?

Sources

Barker, E. (2016, August 9). 6 science-backed tips for boosting your creativity. *The Week.* https://theweek.com/articles/640778/6-sciencebacked-tips-boosting-creativity

da Costa, S., Páez, D., Sánchez, F., Garaigordobil, M., & Gondim, S. (2015). Personal factors of creativity: A second order meta-analysis. *Journal of Work and Organizational Psychology, 31*(3), 165–173. https://doi.org/10.1016/j.rpto.2015.06.002

McLean, T. (2019, September 11). *What do lucky people do differently?* [video]. BBC Reel. https://www.bbc.com/reel/video/p07khzdh/what-do-lucky-people-do-differently-

Morrice, P. (2019 December/2020 January). Teaching moment. *Golf Digest.* See pp. 62–66.

Osborn, A. F. (1963). *Applied imagination* (3rd revised ed.). Charles Scribner's Sons. See p. 330 for quotation.

Shermer, M. (2006). As luck would have it. *Scientific American, 294*(4), 35. https://doi.org/10.1038/scientificamerican0406-35

Chapter 36

CQ: How Can an Expected Outcome Be Changed for the Better?

CPS: I loved the game of baseball as a child, and I clearly remember the opening practice of my first team, the Panthers. Our coach was an enthusiastic college professor and the father of my best friend. After the first part of practice, he told the veteran 9-year-old players to go home. The new players, the rookie 8-year-olds, were taken aside for a lecture. "I want to teach you an important word," said the coach. "It's called 'anticipate,' and it's very important in baseball." As a fielder, one always has to know where to go depending on where the ball is hit. To this day, I still thank Coach Diehl for this important lesson about baseball—and creativity.

The brain constantly anticipates in life, scanning the environment for cues about how things will go. While traveling overseas, I once saw a line of greeting cards where the front image showed an expected outcome. For instance, two cave people were approaching each other with a club. In opening the card, I expected a fight. To the contrary, the inside image showed the two men extending their hands in friendship. (Please see baerenpresse.de for information about these cards.)

Niran Jeyanesan provided a different ending to a story in Canada. Jeyanesan, a Toronto constable, received a call about an 18-year-old man shoplifting a dress shirt, tie, and socks at a local Walmart. The young man had an upcoming job interview, and, faced with his father's illness and limited resources, wanted to help his family economically.

The anticipated outcome would have been an arrest. Yet, after hearing the shoplifter's story, Constable Jeyanesan did the opposite. He bought clothes for the young man in preparation for the interview. Not only did he wear the shirt and tie to the interview, but he also landed the job and started it shortly after the shoplifting episode.

The ending gets better: Others heard of the story and aided the young man's father in gaining employment.

SCAMPER code: Reverse. Constable Jeyanesan's reversal of expectations allowed for a creative outcome that benefited the young man and his family.

Question for creative thought: The word of the day is "eucastrophe." (Yes, it is actually a word, meaning a sudden and positive ending in a story.) Find a story—an actual one is preferred—where a eucatastrophic resolution happened in a way similar to the story above. What factor(s) played a part in the unexpectedly favorable ending?

Source

BBC News. (2017, August 12). *Toronto shoplifter gets job after policeman bought him interview shirt*. https://www.bbc.com/news/world-us-canada-40914118

Chapter 37

CQ: How Can I See The World in a Different Way?

CPS: Assuming that a person sleeps 8 hours a day, a tremendous amount is seen in the remaining 16 hours: the commute to work, playing with kids, walking in the park, and having coffee with a friend. But is it really? According to Rodolfo Llinas, a neuroscientist at the New York University School of Medicine, people may not "see" much of the world; rather, they project onto it. In other words, data from the "outside" world composes about 20% of the perspectives that we form. The other 80% consists of our minds filling in the gaps. The same idea holds true in a psychotherapeutic approach called cognitive-behavioral therapy, which claims that we interpret what we view in the world based on our beliefs. What's important is not the event itself, but how we "see" it.

According to creativity expert Keith Sawyer, one cure to breaking out of this daily pattern is to take mini-trips by going to places like hobby shops, train stations, and museums—really any place "crammed with physical objects." He suggests looking not for shopping purposes, but for inspiration.

This type of inspiration struck Howard Schultz, a person who may influence your life every day. While working in marketing for Starbucks, Schultz visited Milan in 1983 and saw an espresso bar for the first time. He returned to Seattle with the idea of starting one there. The Starbucks owners offered seed money to develop the idea. Though 300 customers filed in the first day, some feedback was less than positive. He made subsequent changes, drew upwards of a thousand customers daily, and went on to buy out Starbucks. Without the Milan visit, the creative spark for the current Starbucks stores may not have occurred.

Michalko identifies one example of how trip-taking resulted in a candy from the early 1900s. George Smith was dedicated to making his candy on a stick different than others. He went to the racetrack and bet a considerable amount of money on a horse that ended up winning. The horse's name? Lolly Pop. He kept the same name for his candy and consequently made history.

SCAMPER code: Modify. Observing and building upon things you see in your travels, whether it be in your neighborhood or another country, can lead to creative applications.

Question for creative thought: Trip-taking can be done from your computer or nearby library. Find a magazine, such as *National Geographic*, or a website on life in a different country. Watch a travel show. You may inevitably focus on what is different. How can those differences inspire you to add creative zest in your own life?

Sources

Michalko, M. (2006). *Thinkertoys: A handbook of creative-thinking techniques* (2nd ed.). Ten Speed Press. See p.18.

Sawyer, K. (2013). *Zig zag: A surprising path to greater creativity*. Wiley. See p. 89 for direct quote.

Chapter 38

CQ: What Could Prevent a Person from Stealing a Bicycle?

CPS: Visit certain cities around the world, and you'll immediately notice the prevalence of a certain form of transportation: Bicycles seem to be everywhere. Utrecht, a major city in the Netherlands, expects two times the number of bike commuters in the next 10 years, and 33,000 parking spaces for bicycles will be found there. Vienna has added 5,000 additional bike spaces; Berlin's plan forecasts 100,000 new spaces. Helsinki has 800 miles of bike paths for residents. Bogotá's commuter rate by bike increased from 6% to 9% from 2017 to 2019 alone. Nearly two-thirds of Copenhagen residents pedal to school or the workplace. One resident said that she doesn't think that she has driven a car over the past 15 years and compared cycling to "getting dressed or brushing your teeth in the morning...biking is what we do."

Though these developments certainly have benefits, with more bikes around, the need for bike protection also escalates. San Francisco had an estimated 4,085 bicycle thefts in 2014, so one company there designed a creative way to deter the temptation. "SkunkLock" is a bicycle lock that emits a foul-smelling gas if a person attempts to steal a bike secured by it. The gas prompts shortness of breath and vision problems for would-be thieves, ruining their clothing in the process. The lock has been dubbed "The Lock that Fights Back."

Michalko outlined patented items that perhaps weren't the best of ideas—a diaper for parakeets, an alarm that sprays water on sleepers' faces, and a golf ball that emits smoke to aid in finding it. This gas-emitting idea may be different, however, as crowdfunding efforts for SkunkLock collected over $8,000 toward its $20,000 goal on the initial day. Four years later, the young company continues to fill orders for a second, further improved version of SkunkLock.

SCAMPER code: Modify. Consider how many ways the bicycle lock could be modified. Making a lock from tougher material has been an approach over the years. The gas emission, for better or worse, is one way to deter a would-be thief.

Question for creative thought: Seelig discussed how absurd ideas can lead to fascinating ones. She asked students to develop their worst ideas in facing life challenges, then to brainstorm how to actually implement those ideas. In her example, students wanted to travel the globe, yet lacked money to do it. A "worst" idea was getting a jet on layaway as a way to postpone costs. In the subsequent creative brainstorm, students developed a reality show concept where, in each episode, a group would travel to various countries to start businesses. What would be a "worst" idea for a challenge in your life, and how could it be modified to become viable?

Sources

BBC News. (2016, October 21). *Chemical bike lock causes vomiting to deter thieves*. https://www.bbc.com/news/world-us-canada-37732748

Kirschbaum, P. (2019, August 8). Copenhagen has taken bicycle commuting to a whole new level. *Los Angeles Times*. https://www.latimes.com/world-nation/story/2019-08-07/copenhagen-has-taken-bicycle-commuting-to-a-new-level

Michalko, M. (2006). *Thinkertoys: A handbook of creative-thinking techniques* (2nd ed.). Ten Speed Press.

Peters, A. (2019, June 27). *These are the 20 best cities for biking in the world*. Fast Company. https://www.fastcompany.com/90367664/these-are-the-20-best-cities-for-biking-in-the-world

Seelig, T. (2015). *Insight out: Get ideas out of your head and into the world*. HarperOne.

SkunkLock. (2020). *The only lock that fights back*. https://www.skunklock.com/homepage2

Chapter 39

CQ: How Can Prison Time Be More Worthwhile?

CPS: Generally the words "prison" and "creativity" don't go together, but a look at certain ideas, both outside the United States, may change that perspective.

Take Sofia Niño de Rivera, a top comedian in Latin America, who offered 10 workshops on stand-up comedy to female inmates at Mexico's Santa Martha Acatitla penitentiary in 2017. The hope was to aid the women's mental health. The comedian commented, "Women in prison don't have a lot of tools to help them handle emotional issues. I think stand-up is something that can help them." In a corrupt system with limited mental healthcare access, the workshops were a success, leading to more programs planned for both women and men in other facilities. One prison official noted a more positive attitude among inmates, adding that their "new outlook on life is contagious."

The Netherlands was facing a problem opposite from what many other countries face: fewer people in prisons. The solution? Import them. The government arranged to accept 240 prisoners from Norway to maintain its population in correctional facilities. Moreover, in some Dutch prisons, inmates are handed keys to their own cells for entry and exit before 9:30 p.m. Despite criticism, the government maintains that the plan provides prisoners more responsibility.

Finally, can solitary confinement have its advantages? One former prosecutor in South Korea thought so. Kwon Yong-suk worked nearly 100 hours a week for six months and began to wonder if solitary confinement might be an improvement over his long work grind. He talked to a friend, a prison warden, about the possibility of voluntarily staying in an actual jail cell. There's too much red tape to do this, he was told. Instead, the lawyer opened a prison-oriented retreat where visitors are "locked away" by themselves for 20 hours a day over two days, helping them find some quiet in life. Each cell comes with a diary, a yoga mat, a tea set, and a toilet.

SCAMPER codes: Substitute, Modify, Put to other uses. A comedian substitutes comedy into the mix of a prison experience. A correctional facility is modified through adding prisoners from another country and encouraging inmate responsibilities through giving them keys to their cells. Taking the solitary confinement concept and making it into a retreat facility is a perfect example of putting an idea to other uses.

Question for creative thought: Have you ever heard someone say, "Wow, that really opened my eyes"? Perhaps it was a movie, a lecture, a book, or a podcast that helped them to realize an alternative view. For me, my "creative eyes" are often opened by stories of life in other countries, as reflected in this chapter.

What opens your "creative eyes?" What places prompt your eyes to widen in capturing the creativity at hand? Babineaux and Krumboltz (2013) related that innovation is connected to activity and breaking out of similar patterns in life. They proposed a "Map your Luck" exercise where one can track areas of the same-old, same-old in life and then substitutes them with places where an unanticipated gem in creative thinking may be found. What new activities or places might stimulate your "creative eyes?"

Sources

Ash, L. (2016, November 10). *The Dutch prison crisis: A shortage of prisoners*. BBC News. https://www.bbc.com/news/magazine-37904263

Babineaux, R., & Krumboltz, J. (2013). Fail fast, fail often: How losing can help you win. Jeremy P. Tarcher/Penguin. See pp. 118-119 for the exercise.

Bulman, M. (2017, July 13). *Dutch prisons are giving inmates keys to their cells*. Independent. https://www.independent.co.uk/news/world/europe/dutch-prisons-inmates-keys-cells-netherlands-dordrecht-heerhugowaard-zaandam-arnhem-a7838586.html

Moon, K. (2018, July 2). *A South Korean 'prison' for people seeking peace and quiet* [video]. BBC Worklife. https://www.bbc.com/worklife/article/20180702-a-south-korean-prison-for-people-seeking-peace-and-quiet

Tucker, D. (2017, October 20). *Mexican comedian brings stand-up to female prisoners*. BBC News. https://www.bbc.com/news/world-latin-america-41565813

Chapter 40

CQ: How Can We Detect the Cause of an Airplane Crash?

CPS: We have all heard the tragic story of a passenger plane crash—hundreds are killed, there's a massive effort to find survivors, and we read about the victims' life stories. And then there's always the eventual question: What caused the crash?

David Warren lost his father, a missionary on his way to Australia, in such a crash in 1934. His father's last gift to him was a radio set that Warren loved. Warren went on to earn a Ph.D. in chemistry in London in his 20s, then specialized in rocket science. While working for a branch of Australia's Department of Defence, he was temporarily loaned away to assist in helping to solve a puzzle: Why did a certain model of British airliner, the first commercial plane in the world, repeatedly crash?

Various reasons were proposed, and one of them sparked Warren's thinking. If a plane were hijacked and subsequently crashed, wouldn't it be helpful to have some type of mini-recorder onboard to capture the pilots' communication? Around the same time, Warren visited a trade show in Sydney and became fascinated with the Miniphon, the world's first dictation device being marketed to business people. "There'd been nothing before like it," Warren said later.

What if, he wondered, something like this Miniphon were installed on an airplane to record communication? Sharing the idea with his boss hit resistance, as Warren was reminded that he was a chemist. The idea, after all, had nothing to do with his field.

Warren persisted, later pitching his idea to a new boss who approved it only if Warren worked on the project in secret. He wrote up the idea in a report and distributed it to others in the airline industry. The pilots' union strongly resisted, describing it as a secretive device and claiming that "no plane would take off in Australia with Big Brother listening." Other authorities in civil aviation also dismissed the idea, branding it as insignificant. Warren still persisted, building a prototype, getting support from a higher-up, and subsequently getting an enthusiastic reception in England. (En route to London, ironically, Warren's plane had mechanical difficulties, as an engine failed over the Mediterranean Sea. The pilots managed to land safely, however.) Australia later became the initial country to mandate voice recorders on airplanes in 1960.

SCAMPER code: Put to other uses. For Dr. Warren, the dictation device he saw at the trade fair had a clear application in the airline industry.

Question for creative thought: Consider the innovation behind a dictation device that Dr. Warren adapted so brilliantly in this story. Many mobile phones have a similar type of voice memo feature, which is one way to capture ideas that you want to ensure are kept. What are other ways that creative ideas can be safeguarded?

Source

Seales, R. (2019, July 18). *This little-known inventor has probably saved your life*. BBC News. https://www.bbc.com/news/world-australia-49012771

Chapter 41

CQ: How Can People Be Encouraged to Buy a Used Car?

CPS: We encounter commercials on nearly every screen: standard television, movie theaters, gas station pumps, and YouTube. If those commercials persuade people to buy something—a new car, a new refrigerator, or a new computer—then why not convince them to buy something that, ordinarily, they have absolutely no interest in purchasing?

Like a used car. A specific one. A 1996 Honda Accord with 141,095 miles.

The price started out at $499, though it only escalated in value after Max Lanman's video appeared. The car, owned by his girlfriend, was featured in his professional commercial of the otherwise mundane car. Lanman, a filmmaker by occupation, hired a female Los Angeles actor to drive the car named "Greenie." The commercial was sure to include a close-up shot of the tape deck, a feature seen as antique by modern viewers.

Other car commercials—for new models, mind you—have scenic backdrops. Lanman's video was no different. In fact, the idea was sparked during a drive on Highway 1 near Los Angeles. "It dawned on me that it would be really funny to film a car commercial for a really crappy car against such a gorgeous backdrop," he said.

The idea worked. One eBay bid came in at over $100,000. Not bad for a "crappy" car called "Greenie."

The sale of Greenie reminds me of a personal story: While in high school, my brother—yes, the same brother to whom this book is dedicated—placed a classified ad in our town newspaper for a used car. Mind you, my brother didn't actually *own* a car. In fact, he may not have even passed his driver's test at that point. The car belonged to one of his high school teachers, specifically his driver's education teacher. "I think the teacher got some pretty good offers by 8 o'clock that night," my brother said years later, still chuckling when he recalled the prank. My parents were not amused, though something tells me that they laughed at the practical joke behind our backs.

SCAMPER code: Adapt. Borrowing the format for a new car commercial, complete with a professional voiceover, can draw interest for a car that has already seen many, many miles.

Question for creative thought: Write a "for sale" advertisement for an obscure item within eyesight—a pen that you got from the local bank, a book from 2004, or perhaps a half-full bottle of hand sanitizer. What would you write to entice interest in it?

Source

BBC News. (2017, November 4). *Price soars after filmmaker's spoof used car ad goes viral*. https://www.bbc.com/news/world-us-canada-41871936

Chapter 42

CQ: If We Can Locate Satellites from Earth, Can We Locate Earth Objects from Space?

CPS: Many people may be hard-pressed to know what GPS (global positioning system) stands for, but it certainly has an effect on their lives. Lose your phone? GPS to the rescue. Did your young driver make it safely to school? GPS is there. Interested in seeing your friend's new home 3,000 miles away? GPS can show it to you.

Johnson described how GPS was formulated through a flipped question. In 1958, two physicists at the Applied Physics Laboratory at the Johns Hopkins University were posed a question: If a location on the ground could locate a satellite, could the reverse process also occur? In other words, could a satellite identify a location on earth? After a few days of analysis, they concluded that it could. Originally called the Transit system, GPS came to the public in 1983 by President Reagan, and now dozens of satellites guide our GPS-oriented lives.

Traffic navigation is a common application for GPS, but it also has life-changing uses. The GoodSAM app pairs cardiac arrest emergency calls with responders' locations to facilitate help, particularly given the difficulty that ambulance and other response vehicles have in getting through London's traffic. Accredited individuals in first aid can join the app, and at least 10,000 people in the United Kingdom have already done so.

A 2017 BBC video story described a woman who saved a man whose heart had stopped beating. She was several blocks away when he collapsed, yet, thanks to the app, arrived four minutes before paramedics, saving precious time in first aid. After starting CPR and applying a defibrillator, the man came to consciousness. "I'll never forget it," she said. "Never forget that moment at all."

Also used in parts of Australia and the United States, this app appears to be saving lives, all because of the flipped question asked over 50 years ago.

SCAMPER code: Reverse. Reversing the satellite model to assist with Earth location has led to numerous applications that truly assist in life.

Question for creative thought: The power of reversal in ideation can be profound. For instance, you can begin by writing the ending of a book. Planning your future? Write the next chapter of your "planned life." Write the final paragraph first, then go back to the beginning and explain how you got to the end success. What was the process like?

Sources

GoodSAM. (2020). *Instant location/video/consultation*. https://www.goodsamapp.org/

Holland, N. (2017, December 19). *App can get first aider to you faster than an ambulance* [video]. BBC News. https://www.bbc.com/news/av/stories-42397008/app-can-get-first-aider-to-you-faster-than-an-ambulance

Johnson, S. (2010). *Where good ideas come from*. Riverhead Books.

Chapter 43

CQ: How Do I Find the Person of My Dreams?

CPS: Imagine being a man who would like to marry a woman, but who also lacks skills in dating. Your parents had an arranged marriage, and the pressure from them to marry is only increasing. Your high school had a strict policy against males interacting with females. At 27, you have not been on a single date. Finally, you live in a country where single men far outnumber single women.

That was one person's case in China, and he knew that his situation was not an isolated one. "Many times, it's not that there's something wrong with us. It's that we don't know what details to pay attention to," he said.

The young man turned to a dating school, the "Fall in Love Emotional Education" dating school in a university apartment in an eastern Chinese city. The school, started in 2014, has 300 students and boasts of a 90% success rate. That is, the vast majority of men are in a dating relationship by the time they graduate. Online dating courses are US $45, and individual coaching can cost around US $3,000. Other dating schools can be found throughout China.

At another school, where male clients range from 18 to 59, one of the typical services includes a makeover to enhance one's social presence. Dance lessons can be another component, as one dating school director found an analogy between dance and dating. "Dating is like a partner dance," he observed. "Sometimes you need to pull. Sometimes you need to push away. Only when you find the right pace you can have a beautiful dance."

SCAMPER code: Put to other uses. If schools can teach academics, can't they also help men learn dating skills?

Question for creative thought: My first formal teaching position occurred at the age of 25 when I walked into the classroom of a private English school in Taiwan. I undoubtedly questioned my teaching skills, but I did have one unique skillset in that situation: English-speaking skills. The question of "What's your superpower?" has been discussed in various forums. In a BBC video, one 11-year-old boy with ADHD described the disorder as a superpower, noting that it helps him to "think outside the box." What is *your* superpower, or, perhaps better phrased, what *are* your superpowers?

Sources

Brown, R. (2019, March 20). *The good things about ADHD: 'It's my superpower.'* BBC News. https://www.bbc.com/news/av/stories-47630021/the-good-things-about-adhd-it-s-my-superpower

Wee, S. L. (2017, November 18). In China, an education on dating. *The New York Times.* https://www.nytimes.com/2017/11/18/business/china-dating-schools.html?_r=0

Yu, R. (2018, May 18). *A dating school for China's many men* [video]. BBC Worklife. https://www.bbc.com/worklife/article/20180521-a-dating-school-for-chinas-many-men

Chapter 44

CQ: What Can I Learn from the Efficiency of a Pit Crew?

CPS: Someone in my childhood group of friends had a great idea one summer: Let's have a mock Indianapolis 500 race on our bikes. The first person to finish 50 laps on a local street would be the winner. I finished the race—not the winner—and remember feeling sick that night, likely a product of dehydration. Water stops weren't a part of this Indy 500. Looking back, I realize that I lacked a key component of race success: a pit crew.

The team in the pit fuels a race car's success by attending to every precise detail of the driver's and the car's performance. Seconds, even milliseconds, matter, and that same value of efficiency is inherent in other areas. James C. Loden, MD, wrote of its importance in operating rooms. "To be efficient," he observed, "your surgery center staff needs to function like a well-disciplined NASCAR pit crew." He reasoned that seconds matter, both in the ways that pit crews refuel and change the tires of a race car as well as minutes of patient time during an office visit.

Dr. Loden is right, at least according to businesses seeking pit crew expertise. In England, the McLaren Technology Group is well known for its accomplishments in the top tiers of racing, and the Oxford University Hospitals sought to utilize its problem-solving abilities in improving treatment. Using McLaren's simulation in healthcare was described as a "complete revelation" by one person at Oxford, who added that its use of data collection and analysis would represent a paradigm shift. Through this precise information, better courses of action can be determined. For example, one idea from clinical trials is for patients to wear sensors post-surgery to better assess outcomes.

The airline industry, oriented toward efficiency in keeping planes in the air, also employs pit crew skills. United Airlines routinely sends ramp leaders for NASCAR training in North Carolina. One United employee noted the strong similarity in their work and pit crews' goals, as both are geared toward safety and rapidity. "Who wouldn't like this?" one United employee asked at the training. "I'm a ramp lead out there, and I'm just really excited to take these skills that I've learned here back home."

SCAMPER code: Adapt. Race car driving seems totally unrelated to operating room procedures, post-surgical care, and airline efficiency, yet applying its pit crew model has a positive impact.

Questions for creative thought: Congratulations! You have just been hired to be on a pit crew. Better yet, you can decide what part of the crew to join. Even if you know little about cars (as I do!), where would your skills best fit with the mission? Assessing the weather conditions? Communicating with the driver? Changing the tires? To draw upon this idea further, who in your life would you assign for other pit crew duties?

Sources

Carney, D. (2015, March 28). *McLaren and medicine: An unlikely pairing*. BBC Autos. http://www.bbc.com/autos/story/20150327-mclaren-weve-got-a-file-on-you

Loden, J. C. (2016, May 1). Turn your OR staff into a pit crew. *Ophthalmology Management*, *20*, 60, 61, 78. https://www.ophthalmologymanagement.com/issues/2016/may-2016/turn-your-or-staff-into-a-pit-crew

Seyler, M., & Kaji, M. (2019, June 6). *United Airlines turns to NASCAR pit crews for quicker turnover*. ABC News. https://abcnews.go.com/amp/Politics/united-airlines-turns-nascar-pit-crews-quicker-turnover/story?id=63403177

Chapter 45

CQ: How Can an Elderly Person Find a Home Away from Home?

CPS: This problem will only become more challenging in terms of numbers. Nearly six million people suffer from its symptoms each day. It is the sixth leading cause of death in the United States, and more seniors pass away from it than two common cancers, breast and prostate, combined. The prognosis nationally is less than favorable, as almost 14 million Americans may be diagnosed with it by 2050. It is Alzheimer's disease.

As of 2016, about half of nursing home residents are victims to the disease, and administrators at some care facilities are creatively attending to their needs as well as the needs of other residents. A care home in Bradford, England, made "travel" easier, by building a train car and ticket office to give residents the simulation of moving by railway. Individuals can eat in first-class comfort, and nearby monitors display footage from the countryside to enhance the experience. One couple, unable to travel by a real train, celebrated their 60-year wedding anniversary on the passenger car. The administrator of the care home said that the idea has given a "new lease on life" for some residents.

A memory care facility in Ohio went even further in adding touches of home, including carpet that smells like grass, a digital sky that darkens during evening hours, and a revamped design that features "homes," not rooms, on a "street" that could be similar to residents' childhoods. Nature sounds are played overhead. It's all about the environment and making it as "homelike" as possible.

SCAMPER code: Modify. Adjusting care facilities by appealing to the senses (sight, sound, etc.) is hoped to have an effect on residents' life satisfaction and well-being.

Questions for creative thought: More and more United States adults face the challenge of caring for aging parents. How else could care homes be modified to help older adults? How can your place of work be modified to improve employee morale or customer satisfaction?

Sources

Alzheimer's Association. (n.d.) *Quick facts*. https://www.alz.org/alzheimers-dementia/facts-figures

BBC News. (2019, February 23). *Bradford care home turns room into train carriage*. https://www.bbc.com/news/av/uk-england-leeds-47333271/bradford-care-home-turns-room-into-train-carriage

Centers for Disease Control. (n.d.). *Alzheimer disease*. https://www.cdc.gov/nchs/fastats/alzheimers.htm

Porter, E. (2016, September 8). *One man turned nursing home design on its head when he created this stunning facility*. Upworthy. https://www.upworthy.com/one-man-turned-nursing-home-design-on-its-head-when-he-created-this-stunning-facility

de Quetteville, H. (2008, June 3). Fake bus stop keeps Alzheimer's patients from wandering off. *The Telegraph*. https://www.telegraph.co.uk/news/newstopics/howaboutthat/2071319/Fake-bus-stop-keeps-Alzheimers-patients-from-wandering-off.html

Stempniak, M. (2019, April 4). *Nursing home creates fake passenger train to create real thrills for residents*. McKnight's Long-Term Care News. https://www.mcknights.com/news/the-brighter-side/nursing-home-creates-fake-passenger-train-to-create-real-thrills-for-residents/

Chapter 46

CQ: How Can Depression Be Addressed in a Community with Limited Resources?

CPS: Constraints get in the way of being creative. True? Actually, not so true—research has shown the opposite to be more accurate. Constraints can help with creativity, as long as they are the proper constraints. Haught-Tromp found support for this idea and also described one example of constraints with the *Green Eggs and Ham* hypothesis. Theodore Geisel, also known as Dr. Seuss, wrote this famed book in 1960 from a publisher's challenge. Write a children's story, the publisher asked, with the same 50 words or fewer. Dr. Seuss rose to the challenge. According to *The Washington Post*, about 17.5 million copies of this constraint-based book are in existence.

Dixon Chibanda, a psychiatrist in Zimbabwe, faced the challenge of battling depression in a country with many constraints: limited mental resources, few fellow psychiatrists, limited space, and nurses contending with other difficulties. As director of the African Mental Health Research Initiative and an associate professor of psychiatry at the University of Zimbabwe, Dr. Chibanda himself was a scarcity in being only one of 12 psychiatrists in the country. In seeking help for those suffering from depression, he was told that the only possible resources were 14 grandmothers and space outside of the building where he worked.

Taking what was available, Dr. Chibanda trained the grandmothers in talk therapy where they offer assistance on benches in the community. Over 400 grandmothers have volunteered to join the Friendship Bench program since 2006, and an estimated 30,000 people have sought help on the benches. The helpers use an approach supported by the research.

"A lot of people think I'm a genius for thinking of this, but it's not true," Dr. Chibanda told the BBC. "I just had to work with what was there."

The Friendship Bench idea has spread to other countries, including Canada and the United States. Bright orange benches attracted 30,000 New Yorkers seeking help in its inaugural year of 2017. Dr. Chibanda visited New York and noted that similar issues—loneliness, mental healthcare access, and finding out more about treatment—are common in both Harare and New York City. The New York City program also brings its bright orange benches to community events, such as street fairs.

Yellow benches are used in Canadian schools, both secondary and post-secondary, for mental health, serving as a vehicle for conversations with peers about seeking help and reducing stigma around it.

SCAMPER code: Substitution. Taking what is often informal, superficial talk on a park bench, and substituting it with more focused, mental health-oriented conversations has led to success with Friendship Benches.

Question for creative thought: The story about benches reminds me of the "Little Free Library" concept started by Todd Bol in Hudson, Wisconsin, in 2009. (If unfamiliar with Little Free Libraries, please see the 30-second video on https://littlefreelibrary.org/start/.) His idea has spread to 85 countries. What "seeds" can be planted in your neighborhood to bring smiles to others?

Sources

Dr. Seuss. (1960). *Green eggs and ham*. Random House.

Haught-Tromp, C. (2017). The *Green Eggs and Ham* hypothesis: How constraints facilitate creativity. *Psychology of Aesthetics, Creativity, and the Arts, 11*(1), 10–17. https://doi.org/10.1037/aca0000061

Kelly, M.L. (2018, October 19). Little Free Library creator Todd Bol dies. *NPR*. https://www.npr.org/2018/10/19/658962057/little-free-library-creator-todd-bol-dies

The Lucas Fiorella Friendship Bench. (n.d.). *The friendship bench*. https://thefriendshipbench.org/the-lucas-fiorella-friendship-bench/

Nuwer, R. (2018, October 16). How a bench and a team of grandmothers can tackle depression. *BBC Future*. https://www.bbc.com/future/article/20181015-how-one-bench-and-a-team-of-grandmothers-can-beat-depression

Rosenberg, T. (2019, July 22). Depressed? Here's a bench. Talk to me. *The New York Times*. https://www.nytimes.com/2019/07/22/opinion/depressed-heres-a-bench-talk-to-me.html?smid=nytcore-ios-share

Sawyer, K. (2013). *Zig zag: A surprising path to greater creativity*. Wiley.

The Washington Post. (2015, July 22). *The best-selling Dr. Seuss books of all time*. https://www.washingtonpost.com/lifestyle/style/the-top-five-best-selling-dr-seuss-books-of-all-time/2015/07/22/129a5ec4-3091-11e5-97ae-30a30cca95d7_gallery.html

Chapter 47

CQ: How Can Time Be Reversed?

CPS: Some readers may recall the song "Back in Time" by Huey Lewis and the News. It was featured in the 1985 film "Back to the Future," the highest grossing film that year. Carl "Rollie" Stichweh may relate to the song, though his connection to it would date to 1963. As the quarterback of the Army football team that year, he was a part of a historic moment—not in football history per se, as his team lost to Navy, 21–15, that day. Rather, Stichweh's moment was monumental in sports television production. His touchdown with 6:19 left in the fourth quarter confused television viewers because Tony Verna, the CBS director overseeing the telecast, tried something for the very first time: instant replay.

Verna wasn't sure it would work. He had found a way to re-cue a tape in 15 seconds instead of the 15 minutes that networks generally needed at the time. Verna tried 30 times to show a replay that day, and each attempt had been aborted. The young director was taping over an old *I Love Lucy* show, and, in one of the failures, Lucille Ball's face could be seen on the football field.

CBS didn't promote the new technology before the game. In fact, the announcer, Lindsey Nelson, was concerned that it would confuse viewers. Immediately after that first replay, he said, "Ladies and gentlemen, Army has not scored again." Perhaps that wasn't enough to quell uncertainty. According to Stichweh, the CBS switchboard was flooded by viewers asking if Army had indeed scored again on the very same play.

The fourth quarter replay ended up being the only one of the game. If interested in seeing a replay of the replay, you may be disappointed:

No tape of it was made, and this moment in sports production was lost forever.

SCAMPER code: Reverse. Going backward in time is the crux of instant replays, allowing sports fans to dissect plays in minute detail and perhaps settle disagreements about whether that play was *really* a touchdown.

Questions for creative thought: Pretend that you were watching the 1963 football game described in this story. Imagine your possible reaction to that fourth quarter replay. Would your initial reaction have been, "This is great!" or "This instant replay is the worst . . ." or somewhere in between? Now transfer the question to today: What is your general reaction to new innovations?

Sources

CBS Sunday morning. (2019, February 3). *Super Bowl: Behind the scenes of instant replays* [video]. https://www.youtube.com/watch?v=EYR1uHoRfe4

Dickey, J. (2013, December 7). Let's review 50 years of instant replay. *Time.* https://ideas.time.com/2013/12/07/lets-review-50-years-of-instant-replay/

Pinter, J. (2015, January 20). *He invented instant replay, the TV trick we now take for granted.* NPR. https://www.npr.org/sections/thetwo-way/2015/01/20/378570541/he-invented-instant-replay-the-tv-trick-we-now-take-for-granted

Songfacts. (n.d.). *Back in Time by Huey Lewis and the News.* https://www.songfacts.com/facts/huey-lewis-the-news/back-in-time

Chapter 48

CQ: How Does Chess Interact with Opportunity in Youth?

CPS: According to Maurice Ashley, a chess player has multiple options in the opening of a match. In fact, the "multiple" is 318 billion different ways, all in just the first four moves. Ashley knows chess. In addition to being a Grandmaster, Ashley was inducted into the US Chess Hall of Fame in 2016. His other accolades are impressive: a three-time national championship coach, an author, and a commentator on ESPN.

Members of the 1991 Raging Rooks chess team, composed of junior high school students from Harlem, also remember Ashley, their young Jamaican-born coach who mastered chess as a teen in Brooklyn. The Raging Rooks were crowned co-champions of the National Junior High Chess Championship that year, beating 60 other teams.

Wait a second. Teens, Harlem, and chess? Teens, Brooklyn, and chess?

Try Nigeria…and Boise.

In Lagos, Nigeria, professional chess player Babatunde Onakoya learned chess as a youth in a poor community, later motivating him to launch the "Chess in Slums" initiative that pairs the game with mentorship. "Learning chess," he commented, "saved me." Onakoya pointed to the benefits in youth learning chess, including patience, strategy, and focus. One youth in the program related that the game "makes me smart" in addition to it boosting his confidence and math skills.

Devin Nakano aims to break the cycle of poverty in part through chessboards in Boise, Idaho. Diagnosed with Asperger's syndrome at age 3, Nakano recalled how physicians informed his mother that his success later in life would be limited. After earning a master's degree in engineering and cybersecurity, he wanted to offer area youth an opportunity through his nonprofit, Y STEM and Chess Inc. While sitting next to a chessboard, Nakano listed some of the benefits that he has seen in helping youth, part of which include critical thinking and communication skills. One teen in the program added even more perspective by saying that chess taught him an important life lesson: "Think of what moves you're going to make ahead of time. That way the moves you make now don't hinder what you can do in the future."

SCAMPER code: Put to other uses. Taking chess to environments where youth may lack resources is one effective way to build skills for a successful future.

Question for creative thought: Write down three hobbies, games, or sports, then jot down six contexts, places, or environments (for example, nursing homes or grocery stores). Match one of the items on the first list with the second list. What creative applications did you just generate?

Sources

Maurice Ashley. (n.d.). *About Maurice Ashley International Grandmaster*. https://mauriceashley.com/about/

BBC News. (2019, March 12). *How chess in Nigeria's slums is changing young lives*. https://www.nytimes.com/1991/04/26/nyregion/harlem-teen-agers-checkmate-a-stereotype.html

O'Hara, M. (2020, February 3). *Boise man with Asperger syndrome starts nonprofit to bring chess and STEM education to underprivileged kids*. KTVB7. https://www.ktvb.com/article/news/local/outreach/sevens-hero/boise-man-with-asberger-syndrome-starts-nonprofit-to-bring-chess-and-stem-education-to-underprivileged-kids/277-63d7c53e-8cc2-4e96-a575-74bb6b8df4e5

TED Ed. (2012). *Working backward to solve problems—Maurice Ashley*. https://ed.ted.com/lessons/working-backward-to-solve-problems-maurice-ashley

Tierney, J. (1991, April 26). Harlem teen-agers checkmate a stereotype. *The New York Times*. https://www.nytimes.com/1991/04/26/nyregion/harlem-teen-agers-checkmate-a-stereotype.html

Chapter 49

CQ: How Can Observation Help Me to Assist Others?

CPS: Observation is not easy, particularly in a world where attention is so often focused on cell phones. Noticing details in the world is secondary to crossing off items on our to-do list and to rushing into the supermarket for bread and milk before dinner. Viewing details in the world often requires a slower pace where the mind can process unnoticed things that, in fact, may have been "seen" numerous times before.

Observation is so critical in innovation that Dyer, Gregersen, and Christensen named it as one of the five key skills of innovation. They noted that innovators are "intense observers," watching the world carefully in regard to how things work—and don't work. In doing so, they are able to "connect common threads across unconnected data."

An expert at making such connections, Milton Erickson was an American psychiatrist known for his creative approaches in working with the unconscious mind. Though diagnosed with polio at the age of 17, he lived a prodigious life before passing away in 1980, specializing in hypnotherapy and writing 140 articles and five books. He saw people as unique and believed that psychotherapy should be geared around each individual person.

O'Hanlon related a story about him that speaks to the uniqueness of people. While in Milwaukee for a guest lecture, Erickson was asked by a colleague to visit a relative who was severely depressed. The elderly woman lived in an old mansion by herself, had never married, and had few relatives. She was confined to a wheelchair due to medical problems, which inhibited her from outside activities. At one point, she was active in her church, though now she attended only on Sundays. As Erickson toured the house, he noticed how old it appeared, as if little had changed since the 1890s. It smelled of must, and the curtains were closed.

The woman, however, saved the pride of her home for the very last part of the tour. In a greenhouse, the woman found great joy in her plant hobby. She was particularly pleased to show her latest project of starting new plants from cuttings of African violets.

After the tour, Erickson told the woman that depression was not her real problem, to which she was quite surprised. The problem, he explained, was that she was letting her money and time go to waste. He suggested finding a list of births, illnesses, and other significant events from the church bulletin and to have her African violets delivered to congregants for condolences, comfort, or congratulations. The woman implemented this idea and, for the next 10 years, became well known in the community as a caring figure with her trademark flower delivery. Upon her death, the obituary in the local paper read, "African Violet Queen of Milwaukee Dies, Mourned by Thousands."

Erickson's keen sense of creative observation changed the woman's life, and, indirectly speaking, inspired a thoughtful contribution to the community in Milwaukee.

SCAMPER code: Put to other uses. Upon Erickson's suggestion, the motive behind the African violets transformed: Instead of merely a hobby, raising the plants became a gift that touched multiple lives. Through observation, he identified a meaningful way to create a positive change.

Questions for creative thought: What "African violets" have you been offered? Would it be worthwhile to let others know your gratitude for the subtle ways they've touched your life?

Sources

The Milton H. Erickson Foundation. (n.d.). *Biography of Milton H. Erickson.* https://www.erickson-foundation.org/biography/

Dyer, J., Gregersen, H., & Christensen, C. M. (2011). *The innovator's DNA: Mastering the five skills of disruptive innovators.* Harvard Business Review Press. See p. 89.

O'Hanlon, B. (1999). *Do one thing different.* William Morrow and Company, Inc.

Chapter 50

CQ: How Might a Compliment Alter a Stressful Situation?

CPS: What is the greatest compliment that you have ever received? How did it brighten your day? Your life? Compliments are a central part to an approach in counseling called solution-focused brief therapy. In this model, compliments can be an effective way to uncover a person's strengths and successes. They can entail the observation that Erickson displayed in the last story, particularly in spotting details. The following story banks on a compliment—a creative one at that—that may have saved a woman's life.

Imagine this horrendous scene: You are biking when a car hits you. The driver proceeds to beat you, drag you into his car, and bind and blindfold you before driving you to a house where you are placed in a closet before blacking out.

Nathalie Birli, a 27-year-old triathlete and mother of a 14-week-old infant, found herself in this dreadful situation while biking in her community in southern Austria. Despite a fractured skull and a broken arm and enduring further physical assaults, Birli made a relatively simple comment during a moment absent of beatings or threats. She complimented the man on his orchids. "I just threw it out there, that his orchids were so beautiful," she said in a *New York Times* story. She told him that she too had orchids and was aware of the necessary care to keep such plants healthy.

The compliment appeared to change everything for Birli, who described how her attacker at that point became "a completely different person." The conversation moved from the orchids to how he had owned many cats that were removed from his care to his difficulties in dating to his mother who was alcoholic. Birli explained that she too was a mother of a young son, asking the man how his life would have been different without his mother.

In the end, Birli arrived home, driven by the man who had kidnapped her. He was later arrested and confessed to the crime. The frightening episode had a positive outcome in large part due to her noticing a rather small detail during a harrowing moment in her life.

SCAMPER code: Adapt. Adapting to the situation seemed to be paramount to Birli's survival. As she told *The New York Times*, "I had to find a way to convince him to trust me." The compliment appears to have been the bridge that saved her.

Questions for creative thought: The concept of inattentional blindness, how little people truly see when their focus is lowered, applies to creativity. Dr. Brian Scholl, a cognitive psychologist, summarized it well: "This research is showing us something that we didn't think was the case—that we can fail to perceive very major things going on right in front of our eyes." If ever possible, sit in the passenger seat while someone else drives you to a place where you have recently driven. What things did you notice that you previously didn't see? In the broader scope of life, what resources may be present in facing a problem-opportunity that were previously unnoticed?

Sources

Carpenter, S. (2001, April). Sights unseen. *Monitor on Psychology, 32*(4), 54. https://www.apa.org/monitor/apr01/blindness. See paragraph 5 for quotation.

De Jong, P., & Berg, I. K. (1998). *Interviewing for solutions*. Brooks/Cole Publishing Company.

Eddy, M. (2019, July 30). She thought he would kill her. Then she complimented his orchids. *The New York Times*. https://www.nytimes.com/2019/07/30/world/europe/austria-cyclist-abducted.html?smid=nytcore-ios-share

Chapter 51

CQ: How Can Art Help Solve Community Problems?

CPS: "Artists can be creative problem-solvers," said Jane Bedell in a *New York Times* article. And why would the assistant commissioner and medical director at a neighborhood health center in New York City be saying this?

Artists and birth outcomes, artists and parenting issues, artists and veterans facing PTSD—New York City has made all these connections. Since 2015, the city's Department of Cultural Affairs has paired artists with public agencies, most recently the Department of Health and Mental Hygiene, the Department of Records and Information Services, the Department of Aging, and the Mayor's Office of Sustainability. On the surface, these certainly appear to be unusual combinations. The Public Artists in Residence (PAIR) program, a part of the city's Department of Cultural Affairs, coordinates the artists' residencies, which are aimed at developing innovative projects around social issues.

"The mission is really to bring the creative energy and intelligence of artists to challenges facing city agencies," explained Tom Finkelpearl, the city's cultural affairs commissioner and the PAIR initiator. One artist-in-residence in a neighborhood health center planned to integrate film and storytelling around healthcare in the Bronx. Past projects by artists have featured war scenes in Greek tragedies to assist homeless veterans suffering from PTSD, as well as a bicycle-driven messenger service for dispersing information about government programs to individuals in predominantly Spanish-speaking neighborhoods.

One person deserving credit for inspiring the PAIR program is Mierle Laderman Ukeles, a ground-breaking artist who did an unsalaried residency with the city's Department of Sanitation. She started her work there shortly after proposing the concept in 1976. One of her projects, the "Touch Sanitation Performance," reflected her year-long work of visits to the districts of the department and shaking hands with all of the 8,500 sanitation workers who were willing to do so.

SCAMPER code: Adapt. Placing artists' talents in other contexts is another tool to address social issues and help people's lives.

Question for creative thought: Take time to notice how art is present in so many places visited daily, including libraries, hair salons, and restaurants. What other places could be brightened through artwork?

Sources

Chow, A. R. (2018, January 23). Beyond murals: New York picks 4 artists in residence to tackle social issues. *The New York Times*. https://www.nytimes.com/2018/01/23/arts/design/nyc-artist-residency-tatyana-fazlalizadeh.html

Haigney, S. (2019, April 5). Artists as "creative problem-solvers" at city agencies. *The New York Times*. https://www.nytimes.com/2019/04/05/arts/design/public-artists-in-residence-new-york.html

Kennedy, R. (2016, September 21). An artist who calls the sanitation department home. *The New York Times*. https://www.nytimes.com/2016/09/22/arts/design/mierle-laderman-ukeles-new-york-city-sanitation-department.html

Chapter 52

Becoming the Innovator Next Door

Before saying goodbye in this book, I want to tell you about flamingos. Yes, flamingos. I once had the joy of seeing them in the wild in Chile and learned a fascinating fact about them. Their primary diet consists of tiny creatures in the water, so one meal requires a lot of consistent work. Interestingly, their feet are vital to eating—they use them to scratch the floor of the lake to uncover their food. It takes more than a quick gulp under the water to fulfill their appetite, and the same point applies to creativity. It takes frequent "scratching" to maintain the neuronal engines of creative thinking. Just like the flamingo looking for lunch, we would go hungry in our creative pursuits if we stopped seeing our worlds with creative lenses. My point of encouragement: Keep scratching!

I will be the first person to acknowledge that these pursuits take time and effort. It may not be easy, particularly at first. Like a flamingo can't satisfy its appetite by scratching in just one small area for a small period of time, people searching for ideas to change their jobs, transform their communities, or find a better path to wellness may come up short.

Adopting a mindset of what Puccio, Mance, and Murdock call "deliberate creativity" takes commitment—commitment to proactively coming up with new ideas. The SCAMPER acronym is just one technique for generating ideas. Many more methods exist, and it may be worth searching them out to help in your scratching process. And remember. That next idea of yours doesn't mean a trip outside of the proverbial box. It could be closer than you think, perhaps somewhere near the edges of the box—the fringes of your creative mind. The innovator next door—

the everyday person trying to get through life a bit differently—doesn't have to be your neighbor. It can be you.

Obstacles? Yes, they will arise. Yet one thing is certain: Your creativity lives today. Allow your creative mindset to inspire your self-care and wellness as well as your contributions to the world. Martin Seligman, a noted psychologist and pioneer in positive psychology, related a story that often comes to my mind when speaking with others, from my own students to ex-strangers who are now new best friends, about their creativity. While having dinner with two respected older figures in his field, Seligman asked them about the point in life when they were most creative. "'*Right now!*' they roared in unison." And so it goes.

The bottom line to this book can be summarized in four words: Creativity lives in you.

Your creativity today and tomorrow will aid your life, and, at the same time, will be a service to your community and to society at large. I truly hope that these stories propel your creative endeavors. Please feel free to keep me posted on your successes, both small and larger than small, at creativestrengths.com@gmail.com.

Sources

Carson, S. (2010). *Your creative brain: Seven steps to maximize imagination, productivity, and innovation in your life*. Jossey-Bass. See p. 291.

Seligman, M. E. P. (2018). *The hope circuit*. PublicAffairs. See p. 360.

Puccio, G. J., Mance, M., & Murdock, M. C. (2011). *Creative leadership: Skills that drive change* (2nd ed.). SAGE.

"Thank you for calling Creative Business Seminars. If you'd like to become a more creative problem solver, press 1 without touching any part of your telephone."

Acknowledgments

My deepest gratitude goes to:

- my wife and daughters for their support and patience with "all of this creativity stuff";
- my colleagues in the Department of Counseling at Indiana University of Pennsylvania, both current and past, with whom it has been a pleasure and honor to work;
- Kendra Williamson, a tremendous editor, for her creativity, thoughtfulness, and foresight;
- Dr. Sam Gladding of Wake Forest University for being an incessant source of encouragement in my work and for his immeasurable contributions to the creativity field;
- Dr. Gemma Jiang of the University of Pittsburgh for her creative insights in helping to craft key parts of the book; and
- Barbara Dee and her team at Suncoast Digital Press for their wisdom and dedication to the completion and publication of this book.

About the Author

Creative thinking + teaching + enthusiasm = John McCarthy, Ph.D.

John McCarthy is on a mission to spark creativity in the classroom and through workshops, articles, blogs, and books. Fascinated by the quick thinking of seven older siblings, John has been drawn to creativity since his childhood in Western New York. His interest in the "outside the ordinary" extended to the playground where his friends quickly improvised plays in football huddles, devised trick shots on the basketball court, and found unusual ways to throw a whiffleball from a pitcher's mound.

By the time that he graduated from high school, he regretfully abandoned his dream of playing second base for the Boston Red Sox and instead studied mass communication at St. Bonaventure University.

His passion about thinking led him to pursue a doctoral degree in counseling psychology. Given his DNA—both parents and siblings were teachers—he encountered the joy of the classroom and never left, teaching for 25+ years and having the ultimate honor of witnessing students' success and growth.

He is a professor in the Department of Counseling at Indiana University of Pennsylvania where he founded and directed the Center for Creativity and Change. He has offered professional presentations on creativity thinking and other mental health-related topics in Turkey, Singapore, Ukraine, Kyrgyzstan, Malaysia, China, Hong Kong, England, Canada, and Taiwan. He also served as an academic visitor at the University of Cambridge in 2011.

McCarthy has 30 journal publications and over 60 professional presentations. His professional writings have been featured in the *Pittsburgh Post-Gazette*, the *Buffalo News, Cleveland.com, Counseling Today*, and the *Psychotherapy Networker*.

He lives in the Pittsburgh area and still secretly hopes for a tryout with the Red Sox. He looks forward to his sixth decade where he hopes to hike in Indonesia and Ethiopia, host a show on PBS, study improv and Mandarin, and continue to marvel at others' creative stories. His blogs can be found at creativestrengths.com.

www.ingramcontent.com/pod-product-compliance
Lightning Source LLC
Chambersburg PA
CBHW030154100526
44592CB00009B/265